Buildings of Medieval Europe

Studies in social and landscape contexts of medieval buildings

Edited by

Duncan Berryman and Sarah Kerr

OXBOW | books
Oxford & Philadelphia

Published in the United Kingdom in 2018 by
OXBOW BOOKS
The Old Music Hall, 106–108 Cowley Road, Oxford OX4 1JE

and in the United States by
OXBOW BOOKS
1950 Lawrence Road, Havertown, PA 19083

Paperback Edition: ISBN 978-1-78570-971-5
Digital Edition: ISBN 978-1-78570-972-2 (epub)

A CIP record for this book is available from the British Library

Library of Congress Control Number: 2018944548

Typeset in India by Versatile PreMedia Services

For a complete list of Oxbow titles, please contact:

UNITED KINGDOM
Oxbow Books
Telephone (01865) 241249, Fax (01865) 794449
Email: oxbow@oxbowbooks.com
www.oxbowbooks.com

UNITED STATES OF AMERICA
Oxbow Books
Telephone (800) 791-9354, Fax (610) 853-9146
Email: queries@casemateacademic.com
www.casemateacademic.com/oxbow

Oxbow Books is part of the Casemate Group

Front cover: Petrapilosa, Croatia, by Josip Višnjić
Back cover: Byzantine style church uncovered in Alba Iulia, Romania, by Daniela Marcu Istrate

Part 1

Britain and Scandinavia

Contents

List of figures

List of contributors

ILARI AALTO
University of Turku, Finland

ROBIN GULLBRANDSSON
Västergötlands Museum, Sweden

MARTIN HUGGON
University of Sheffield, United Kingdom

DANIELA MARCU ISTRATE
'Vasile Pârvan' Institute of Archaeology,
Bucharest, Romania

MIRIAM STEINBORN
Römisch Germanisches Zentralmuseum Mainz,
Germany

PAVEL VAŘEKA
University of West Bohemia, Czech Republic

JOSIP VIŠNJIĆ
Croatian Conservation Institute, Croatia

STUART WHATLEY
Museum of Copenhagen, Denmark

Chapter 1

Introduction

Duncan Berryman and Sarah Kerr

This volume brings together a range of innovative studies of medieval buildings from across Europe. The concept for this work and the resulting papers began life as a session at the 2016 annual conference of the European Archaeological Association in Vilnius, Lithuania. Due to the range and quality of papers it was decided that publication was required to bring the new studies to a wider audience than could fit into the conference room during the session. The intention of the session was to provide a focus for discussion of medieval buildings from an archaeological perspective, particularly presenting new approaches to buildings and highlighting recent excavations and surveys. The majority of papers presented at the session are included in this collection. This volume is the result of considerable interest in the topic and includes papers from across Europe; a particular strength is the contributions from eastern Europe, which is often underrepresented in the literature of western Europe. This book is not a survey of building types across Europe or an in-depth study of European architecture; it aims to be a starting point for wider discussions of medieval buildings. The studies presented here highlight new methods and directions for the discipline and it is hoped that they will stimulate debate within medieval building scholarship. Since the session in 2016, there has been a subsequent session at the 2017 European Archaeological Association in Maastricht, The Netherlands, and similar sessions are planned for future conferences. These sessions and publications provide welcome opportunities to discuss and explore the subject of medieval buildings and expand our knowledge with new discoveries.

The papers in this book have been divided into two parts based on their geographic focus. The first part looks at Scandinavia and Britain; while the second concentrates on central and eastern Europe. This structure brings together complimentary papers and reveals similarities and contrasts across Europe. The papers span a range of social strata, from the upper levels of society and their associated buildings to low-status buildings and common people. The discipline of buildings archaeology is distinct from both archaeology and architectural history, yet connected to both; therefore it is broad in its scope, and a selection of its themes are covered in this volume.

Scholarly research on medieval buildings has favoured high-status examples due to the availability of extant remains above ground and associated documents relating to their construction. The result is a focus on the interpretation of materials, location, and architecture as physical manifestations of wealth, authority, and social status. The discipline in its current stance has moved away from unquantifiable descriptors such as 'status' embracing instead meaning, movement, interaction, and the senses including heat, sound, and sight (e.g. Giles 2007). Whether or not these themes are less abstract than the former is debateable; however, exploring these complex ideas focuses the study on everyday experiences of those associated with buildings, and thus contributes to a better understanding of medieval society. This approach can be described most concisely by Johnson as the study of the 'lived experience' (Johnson 2013, 381), encompassing the shift of emphasis from function to meaning; a theme uniting the papers in this volume.

Medieval buildings are recognised increasingly as among Europe's most significant assets. The discipline of buildings archaeology has grown in-line with this and in doing so includes a more diverse group of contributors including, but not limited to, architectural historians, architects, professional archaeologists, conservators, and academics; the result is a constantly evolving subject and greater interdisciplinarity. Despite the importance of interdisciplinarity, it is not without its problems. A lack of clarity on definitions, theory and common ground is the result of poor communication between disciplines; and this problem persists across all academic research. In archaeology, interdisciplinarity has been most successful in the study of space. The work of Hillier and Hanson (1984; also Hillier 1996), Rapoport (1969; 1990) and Markus (1982) provided the spatial-analysis framework to further the discipline of buildings archaeology. It was adopted eagerly by archaeologists, particularly from 1970s, more readily by prehistorians in these early decades. Spatial analysis is not restricted to the study of buildings, indeed it is often used to analyse artefact distribution; however buildings control and use space more so than any other remnant from the past, consequently spatial analysis is particular relevant to the discipline. Faulkner pioneered the use of spatial analysis in the medieval context in the seminal paper on planning analysis of 14th-century castles (Faulkner 1963). In the 1990s, Fairclough published the key publication on the use of spatial analysis on late medieval castles which delved into the complexities of access; this galvanized the study of space within medieval buildings (Fairclough 1992). Spatial analysis has since been used to study nunneries and monasteries (Gilchrist 1994), urban buildings (King 2009), and noble households (Weikert 2014). Therefore the use of spatial analysis has percolated the discipline of buildings archaeology and now is readily used in the analysis of small, low-status buildings. This has propelled discussions away from the dichotomies of buildings' architecture, such as the vernacular and polite (e.g. Brunskill 2000), military and domestic, the rise and decline. Rather, the contribution of buildings to the understanding of medieval society in now fully recognised and discussions reflect on a broader view of medieval life, including attitudes to authority, privacy and gender (for example Richardson 2003).

Underpinning many of the building interpretations discussed in this volume is the implicit assumption that there was something more fundamental at work in the motivation for creating a structure in a particular way. To discover this the researchers expand their study beyond utilitarian function. The papers included contribute to the current trend of moving away from traditional methods and consider life of those who lived or worked in and around the buildings, alongside the physical structure.

The common theme running through these papers is the role of buildings in the daily lives of medieval people. The studies by Vařeka and Steinborn in Central Europe and Byzantium show how common people lived in both urban and rural contexts and elucidate some elements of their daily lives. The three-compartment house in eastern Central Europe does not have three distinct rooms, rather there are three conceptually different zones and Vařeka's approach explores sub-types based on separation-contact analysis. The one-room house in Serbia has similarly defined zones, as Steinborn assigns dwelling and economic descriptors to guide the discussion and analysis. Each author postulates the difficulties analysing such buildings; however through exploring the extant archaeology the papers deliver an enriched understanding of the medieval people and how their buildings were an integral part of their daily and economic lives.

Three-compartment houses in eastern Central Europe remain in use today, although occupation in these traditional buildings has declined since the 20th century. Building on the extensive archaeological, ethnological, historical and linguistic research undertaken in the last one hundred years on this type of building, Vařeka focuses on the development of the typology. The paper explores the earliest examples of such, comparing attributes and discussing the possibilities of its development, while considering critically the diffusionist explanation versus the autochthonous hypothesis. This geographically and temporally broad paper includes examples from the Slavic cultural tradition of Bohemia and Moravia, Poland, Slovakia, north-eastern Germany, central Germany, north-eastern Bavaria, Austria and Hungary, summarising a large body of work in the process. By discussing the multiple variations of the three-compartment house, Vařeka evaluates the cultural and social significance of the type and the concept of a house as both a dwelling and economic zone, within the broader context of rural housing in Central Europe.

A multi-room or compartment house provides opportunity for a number of methods of analysis, such as access analysis, to determine the specialisation of each space. However, when a small single-celled house is discovered in excavation its possibilities relating to function and use may seem somewhat endless. Steinborn confronts this quandary of spatial ambiguity by using the idea of 'household' as a functionalist strategy in a middle range theoretical approach. The difficulties of analysing a small space and attempting to relate it to medieval society are noted, however Steinborn conveys the connection between the small unit and the wider medieval community. The position of the house, almost pressed against the fortification wall, reveals a change in function of the city itself; while the waste disposal methods within and outside the house may reveal a weak hold of the administrative powers. After evaluating the finds, stratigraphy and wider context, in what may have been the Imperial city *Iustiniana Prima*, Steinborn considers the tendency in archaeological analysis to view space as male-centric due to certain artefacts. It is argued that this humble house with evidence of an attic probably used as accommodation space, could have been occupied by a single person of either sex.

Castles, forts, and hospitals were used rarely by the majority of the population, but for those who lived in them they were the theatre of their daily life. The site of Petropilosa, in the north of the Istrian peninsula in present-day Croatia, developed through the high- to post-medieval period and its excavation revealed a snapshot of life in a feudal fortification. Višnjić's interdisciplinary study of what is described as 'eminently distinguishable development of ... architecture', stratigraphical, artefactual, and historical data, contributes greatly to the knowledge of high medieval Istria. This is an under-studied period of Istria, despite excellent preservation below and above ground; therefore this study furthers the discipline in this area. The complete analysis of the fortress directs focus on life-altering events rather than the daily life of medieval society. A selection of coins, coinciding with a substantial burnt layer have been discussed together with attacks on the fortress cited in historical documents, specifically the conflict between the Aquileian patriarch and Kopar, Count of Gorizia in the 13th century. Višnjić provides an in-depth evaluation of Petropilosa; as a prime example of the feudal fortifications which line the Istrian peninsula, this study is a paragon for the interpretation of the broader area.

The study of high-status buildings contributes a different perspective on medieval life as the focus is often on a single person: a patron, a lord, a king. However, high status buildings had a community which affected their creation, plan and use. Churches were the product of belief and wealth, each element was a display of status usually of the founder; however, in turn they influenced the medieval community. Istrate explores this symbiotic relationship between church and community through focusing on the ruined, multi-phase church uncovered in Alba Iulia, Transylvania. This borderland, between Byzantine Christianity, the steppe and Latin Europe, has a complicated history of occupation and change which altered the community, religion and architecture; the results of which can be seen in the remains of ecclesiastical buildings. As the oldest medieval church discovered north of the Lower Danube the results from the excavation and architectural survey, of what is now St Michael's Roman Catholic Cathedral, offer a detailed insight into the complex multi-ethic and multi-religious Carpathian Basin.

The meeting of different, and at times opposing, cultural powers created areas of unique social, political and cultural relationships which can be identified in the remains of buildings above or below ground. The great powers of Byzantine Christianity and Latin Europe met in Transylvania transforming the area; the results of which are discernible in the rebuilding, altering and destruction of the church in Alba Iulia. Cultural confluences occurred on considerably smaller scales, as small groups travelling between regions created cultural assimilation also discernible in the archaeological record. In the study of medieval roof trusses in Sweden, the cultural connections are not apparent immediately; however Gullbrandsson deliberates the relationships with other Scandinavian practices which may have resulted in the progression away from the timbering technique of *sprättäljning* in the 14th century. Unlike the broad cultural transmission as discussed in Vařeka's and Istrate's papers, this is a small-scale cultural confluence as local craftsmen merged with imported masons, working alongside each other and incorporating the Nordic carpenter traditions with Romanesque roof trusses. Gullbrandsson identifies the influences from other cultures, including France, through the survey of preserved roof trusses dating from the 12th to 14th centuries. The survival of 12th and 13th century roof trusses is of particular importance as they are scarcely preserved outside Scandinavia.

High-status buildings were at times the setting for life-altering, stand-alone events, such as the capture and demolition of Petrapilosa in the 13th century as discussed in Višnjić's paper. Likewise they can be demonstrations of a massive transformation in the community such as religious conversion in Transylvania as described by Istrate. Medieval life could be less volatile even in large-scale, multiple-occupancy medieval buildings as Huggon explores through the study of English hospitals. Once again we see the communication of ideas between cultures evidenced in buildings as the development of English hospitals reveals they were formalised by the Normans in the 11th century then evolved, adding elements of Anglo-Saxon religious and social ideology. This paper builds upon previous studies on medieval buildings and the organisation of space through the discussion of functional spaces and how they interact and relate to each other. Huggon considers the plans of a number of hospitals and how they functioned as both practical buildings and religious spaces, demonstrating the importance of reassessing previously studied buildings through new techniques as the discipline progresses: the result is new interpretations of the English medieval hospital. A framework for understanding hospitals, which often appear to have little in the way of direct similarity, allows a new perspective from which to view them: the intent of those who built them and the result as experienced by those who lived in them. Through analysis of space Huggon postulates the ideological motivations for the organisation of hospitals in particular ways, which surpass restrictions of space and functional requirements. This includes discussion on the imbued meaning within buildings, in which activity and movement is informed and controlled by implicit signs, signals and surfaces.

This subtle influencing, almost lost to the modern audience due to excavation and survival bias, is in contrast to the obscured yet in a way more explicit messages on the Finnish bricks discussed in Aalto's paper. The parallel connecting English medieval hospitals and Finnish bricks is the transfer of meaning from building to audience. Both Aalto and Huggon reflect on the difficulties faced when deciphering these medieval messages. Aalto discusses how in a society in which few people were literate these symbols were indicators of production allowing the brickmakers to quantify, and thus receive payment for, their output. Through the act of drawing into wet brick, identification of who made the brick was clear; however by evaluating the context of signs in the medieval Scandinavia, Aalto discusses the potential secondary meanings, such a devotional prayer.

A number of papers address the relationship between the buildings and the associated community, such as Aalto's analysis of brickmakers' names and the attributes of saints. Huggon's discussion of the community associated with medieval hospitals discovers it was a transect through medieval society; it included the religious and secular, men and women, and the wealthy and poor. Similarly, the harbourside of medieval Copenhagen had a diverse community due to the curious close composition of maritime industrial buildings, elite private housing, administrative buildings, and the royal castle situated to the south. Whatley discusses the results of excavations around the medieval harbour of Copenhagen, which exposed a significant development to facilitate trade before the 15th century. The weighing house was a place in which people worked and spent much of their day, thus providing an insight into their working lives. The community associated with the weighing house lived alongside the elite residents who migrated to take advantage of the high-status goods entering the city. This accelerated Copenhagen's development into a Scandinavian metropolis, evidenced by the rebuilding of the weighing house and associated finds including Chinese porcelain and Portuguese cork.

Civic buildings were constructed to act as central points for trade, controlling taxes and money due to the authorities. Whatley describes how the weighing house had a crucial role in society, and the development, modernisation and expansion of Copenhagen, at a time when the king resided more frequently there from 1400 onwards. There are similar administrative buildings elsewhere in Europe, all of which have associations with the Hanseatic League, demonstrating that Copenhagen was modernising through contacts across Europe, thus becoming a centre of the Scandinavian world.

These papers create new debates in medieval buildings studies and assist the development of new ways to interpret buildings. Many discussions postulate the meaning of the building and at times argue the importance of meaning over function, at least the equal importance of both to understanding the building. As the discipline of medieval buildings studies develops this volume contributes to the understanding of the lived experience.

These studies illuminate new discoveries and recent research from across Europe, bringing it to a wider audience. The study of medieval buildings has a long tradition in archaeology. It is important that its study continues, and these papers give an encouraging picture of the future, as many have been given by early career researchers. It appears that building archaeology has a bright future with many dedicated and enthusiastic scholars.

Acknowledgements

The editors would like to take this opportunity to thank all who contributed to the session in Vilnius, along with the EAA conference organisers who made it possible. We are also grateful to Oxbow for agreeing to publish these papers and for all the support they have provided. And most importantly, we would like to thank the authors who have put in all the hard work to bring these papers to publication. We would also like to note our gratitude to Dr Mark Gardiner, who's enthusiasm and support saw us both complete our PhDs and encouraged our love of medieval buildings.

Bibliography

Brunskill, R. W. (2000) *Vernacular Architecture: An Illustrate Handbook.* London, Faber and Faber.
Fairclough, G. (1992) Meaningful constructions: Spatial and functional analysis of medieval buildings. *Antiquity* 66, 348–366.
Faulkner, P. A. (1963) Castle planning in the fourteenth century. *Archaeological Journal* 120, 215–235.
Gilchrist, R. (1994) *Gender and Material Culture: The Archaeology of Material Culture.* London, Routledge.
Giles, K. (2007) Seeing and believing: Visuality and space in pre-modern England. *World Archaeology* 39 (1), 105–121.
Hillier, B. (1996) *Space is the Machine: A Configurational Theory of Architecture.* Cambridge, Cambridge University Press.
Hillier, B. & Hanson, J. (1984) *The Social Logic of Space.* Cambridge, Cambridge University Press.
King, C. (2009) The interpretation of urban buildings: Power, memory and appropriation in Norwich merchants' houses, *c.* 1400-1660. *World Archaeology* 41 (3), 471–488.
Markus, T. A. (1982) *Order and Space and Society - Architectural Form and its Context in the Scottish Enlightenment.* Edinburgh, Mainstream.
Rapoport, A. (1969) *House Form and Culture.* Princeton, Prentice-Hall.
Rapoport, A. (1990) *History and Precedent in Environmental Design.* Princeton, Prentice-Hall.
Richardson, A. (2003) Gender and space in English royal palaces *c.* 1160 – *c.* 1547: A study in access analysis and imagery. *Medieval Archaeology* 47, 131–166.
Weikert, K. (2014) Place and prestige: Enacting and displaying authority in English domestic spaces during the central Middle Ages. In S. D. Stull (ed.) *From West to East. Current Approaches to Medieval Archaeology*, 96–120. Newcastle upon Tyne, Cambridge Scholars Publishing.

Chapter 2

A key, an axe and a gridiron: Medieval Finnish brickmakers' marks as symbols of identity

Ilari Aalto

The medieval period, *c.* 1150–1520 (Haggrén 2015), saw the introduction of brick as a building material in the Nordic countries. During this period, most of the area of present-day Finland belonged to the Diocese of Åbo (Turku) (Fig. 2.1) which in turn was a part of the Kingdom of Sweden. For one reason or another, some of the brickmakers working in the area of Finland began to inscribe their products with symbols known as brickmakers' marks. The Diocese of Turku will be the geographical scope of this article, as similar brickmakers' marks are not known elsewhere in the medieval Kingdom of Sweden. However, they do appear in neighbouring areas in Russia (Antipov & Gervais 2015) and in the Baltic countries (Ose 2015, 76).

The first brick church in Scandinavia was built in Ringsted in Denmark in 1161, and similar construction projects followed in Sweden in the mid-13th century (Svanberg 2013, 12–13). The art of brickmaking spread in Finland at the end of the same century, and bricks were also made in Estonia (then part of Livonia) in the southern shore of the Baltic Sea in the turn of the 14th century (Bernotas 2013, 148–149; 2017, 22–28; Ratilainen 2014). In the case of the Diocese of Turku it was only in the 15th century that masonry buildings started to be constructed extensively (Uotila 2003, 131; 2009, 306–307; Seppänen 2012, 948–949).

Around one hundred stone church building projects were started, imposing castles were built and in the town of Turku masonry townhouses began to be erected during the peak of medieval masonry building in Finland. The construction works were executed by construction teams that comprised of professional artisans, such as masons and brickmakers (Kuokkanen 1981, 54; Hiekkanen 2003, 30–34; Swanberg 2013). In pace with the increasing construction of masonry buildings, brickmakers are assumed to have adopted a system of marks to sign their production (Rinne 1941,

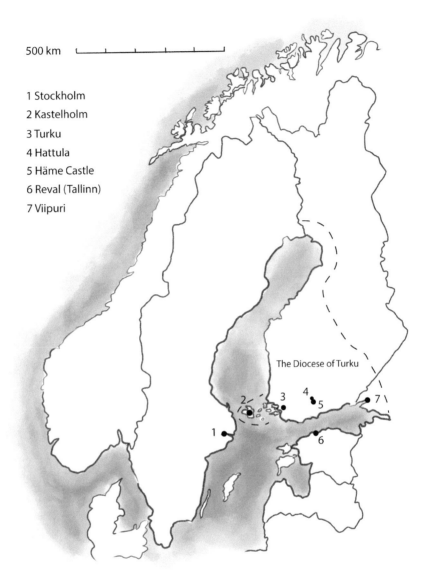

500 km

1 Stockholm
2 Kastelholm
3 Turku
4 Hattula
5 Häme Castle
6 Reval (Tallinn)
7 Viipuri

The Diocese of Turku

Fig. 2.1: The medieval Diocese of Turku and locations mentioned in this paper (Elina Helkala)

309; Venhe 1994; Ratilainen 2012, 27; Aalto 2015; Ose 2015, 76–77). The exact nature of these brickmakers' marks remains unknown.

In Finland, mostly churches, castles and manor houses of the nobility were built of brick and stone. It was only in the last years of the 14th century that private masonry houses began to be built in Turku, the most prominent town in the Eastern Sweden at the time (Uotila 2007; Seppänen 2014; for the earliest use of brick in Turku see

Ratilainen 2014; 2016). During the following century, the Diocese of Turku started to intentionally replace wooden churches with churches built in stone (Hiekkanen 1994; 2007). This meant a remarkable increase in the demand for brick material and skilled workforce that could produce the material and use it to create lasting monuments (Uotila 2009, 306).

The focus of this paper is in the brickmaker's marks, or the symbols brickmakers used to sign their work. Brickmakers' marks were carved in freshly made bricks with a sharp tool before the bricks were left to dry. This separates brickmakers' marks from graffiti, which pilgrims and other churchgoers could have made in bricks after they were fired and already in place in the church wall (e.g. Hiekkanen 2000 and Ratilainen 2011). Both in form and function, brickmakers' marks seem to have much in common with masons' marks known elsewhere in Europe (Alexander 2008). This paper will examine how brickmakers used the marks to express their identity and how the marks are situated in wider medieval imagery. It will focus on a single repeating symbol representing a key that can be seen in different buildings in the region of Finland Proper in southwestern Finland. It will also point out some other marks that have been found in medieval context in the same geographic area.

Although some brickmakers' marks can still be seen *in situ* in medieval churches and castles and are commonly found on archaeological excavations, they remain poorly studied. The first researcher of the subject in Finland was architect Carolus Lindberg, who mentioned the existence of such marks and gave some examples in his doctoral dissertation published in 1919 (Lindberg 1919, 132). Brickmakers' marks in Turku Cathedral were briefly mentioned by archaeologist Juhani Rinne who was responsible for the restoration of Turku Cathedral in the 1920s (Rinne 1941, 309). Leena Venhe has published brickmakers' marks found at the episcopal castle in Kuusisto (Venhe 1994, 37–38). To date, the most thorough study on the matter is a seminar paper written by Tanja Ratilainen in 1997, in which she studied the rich material of brick carvings in Häme Castle (Ratilainen 1997). The author of this paper has also discussed the marked bricks found in medieval context in Aboa Vetus & Ars Nova Museum in Turku (Aalto 2015, see also Ratilainen's comments in Ratilainen 2017). There has only been little discussion about the function of the marks amongst Finnish researchers.

The key – a case study

British antiquarians studying masons' marks in the eighteenth and nineteenth centuries believed that it would be possible to trace the individual craftsmen behind the marks. Hypothetically, this could be possible, but as identical marks could have been used by different masons for several centuries, this approach has not been very successful. Alexander (2008, 30–33) has proposed that it would be more useful to study all the marks in a single building to understand the inner chronology of the marks in that context.

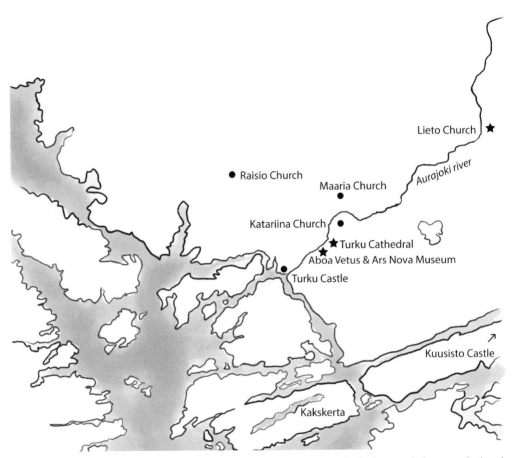

Fig. 2.2: Buildings in Turku region mentioned in the text. Buildings with the key symbol are marked with a star and other buildings mentioned in the text are marked with a circle (Elina Helkala)

Finnish brickmakers' marks form a somewhat different pool of data than the abundance of masons' marks in western Europe. Marks in Finland seem to have been in use for only a short period, possibly only for some generations, and they exist only in small numbers in a limited area. In this perspective, the small quantity of Finnish marks can be an advantage when trying to track the individual artisans, as there is a strong possibility that a single mark was used only by a single brickmaker. One should be cautious, however, when assigning the marks to brickmakers. The pentagram, for example, was a very common apotropaic symbol and house mark in the medieval and early modern period. In the Finnish brick material, this symbol is found at least in Turku Cathedral (Rinne 1941, 309), the episcopal castle in Kuusisto (Venhe 1994, 38) and in a stone house in Aboa Vetus & Ars Nova Museum in Turku (Aalto 2015, 4, fig. 5). Although these structures are temporarily and spatially close enough that a single craftsman could have made the bricks to all the buildings, the general nature of the sign itself makes this impossible to verify. The same symbol has also been found on a 17th-century brick in Louhisaari manor (Ernvall 2017, personal communication, 6 November).

The complete analysis of distribution of the brickmakers' marks in single medieval buildings is not possible in the scope of this paper. Therefore, we will take a case study, and try to track the work of a single itinerant brickmaker, who signed his work with the key symbol (Fig. 2.3, symbol A1). As the material is sporadic and not all medieval churches have yet studied in the research area, thus these results should be seen as a preliminary.

The key symbol in question has been found in several locations (Fig. 2.2) around the town of Turku in southwestern Finland. Precisely the same symbol can be seen in the outer wall of the All Saints Chapel in Turku Cathedral and in the church of St Peter in *Lundo* (Lieto), 11.3 km from Turku Cathedral. The mark was also documented by Lindberg (1919, 31) in Rusko Church, which is situated 9.5 km from the cathedral. The same mark is also known from a brick found in a 15th-century townhouse excavated in Aboa Vetus & Ars Nova Museum in Turku (Aalto 2015, 4, fig. 3).

According to Markus Hiekkanen, the All Saints Chapel was constructed between years 1470–1484 (Hiekkanen 2007, 200), Lieto Church in 1470–1490 (Hiekkanen 2007, 84–85) and Rusko Church between 1510–1530 (Hiekkanen 2007, 156–157). The exact age of the brick found in Aboa Vetus & Ars Nova Museum cannot be deduced, but the brick dates roughly to the 15th or 16th century (Aalto 2015), which corresponds with the other dates. At longest, this would mean a time span of 60 years, which would be an unrealistically long career for a medieval person. At the shortest, however, the time span would be 26 years from 1484 to 1510. A working career of some 30 years seems much more realistic. This gives credibility to the thought that the mark could indeed have belonged to one individual.

The radius of buildings containing the key symbol is well within the limit of one day's travel. This could imply that the working area of a single brickmaker could be geographically rather limited. However, the range of a little over 10 km from Turku Cathedral should be seen as a minimum. It is entirely possible that bricks made by the same artisan could exist in the churches of neighbouring areas, but they have not been found yet. We should not exclude the possibility that an itinerant brickmaker could have worked overseas in mainland Sweden or Livonia as well. It is interesting to note that in Rusko Church there are also two somewhat different symbols (Fig. 2.3, A2–3) representing a key in addition to the symbol discussed here. A brick marked with one of these symbols has also been documented in *Reso* (Raisio) Church, which was constructed in 1500–1520 (Ekko 2008, Raisio no 9 Hiekkanen 2007,

152–154). These marks could represent a younger generation of brickmakers who continued the tradition.

Marks on bricks

Brickmakers' marks are simple designs that were easy to draw on the bricks when the clay was still wet. As symbols, brickmakers' marks can be seen belonging to the group of house marks or owner's marks (*bomärke* in Swedish and *puumerkki* in Finnish), which were personal symbols that were used to sign property (Ekko 1984; for house marks as brickmakers' marks see also Ose 2015, 76). It is characteristic of both the owner's marks and brickmaker's marks that they are simple and easily reproduced, comprising of a limited number of strokes. Several symbols seen in medieval brickmakers' marks remained in use as owner's marks in the post-medieval period.

However, not all markings made in bricks should be considered as brickmakers' marks. Ratilainen (1997, 9–16) has divided symbols on bricks into four different categories: a) representing figures and symbols, b) crosses and criss-crosses, c) numbers and letters and d) other grooves and unclear shapes. Brickmakers' marks can belong to any of Ratilainen's categories a, b or c, but not d. The discerning features for brickmakers' marks are that the symbols are simple enough to draw quickly and to copy precisely and that they have indeed been copied (on masons' marks *cf.* Alexander 2008, 30). The brickmakers' marks are also often cut quite deep in the brick so that they are easily distinguished.

Brickmakers' marks themselves can be divided into four categories based on the themes of symbols. The marks represent a) items, b) abstract, often apotropaic, symbols, c) letters or, more rarely, d) 'actual' owner's marks (Fig. 2.3). Although little systematic documentation of the marks has been conducted in Finland, category a) would seem to be the most common. This category consists mainly of tools and weapons, such as keys, gridirons, axes, hooks, halberdiers and anchors (According to Lindberg [1919, 31] an anchor was drawn on a brick in the medieval church of Lieto on southwestern Finland). Group b) includes St Andrew's cross, pentagrams and swastikas. Group c) seems to be very rare, which is not surprising considering the low level of literacy (Harjula 2008) in the medieval period. Even when used as brickmakers' marks letters do not reveal anything about the literacy of the artisans. A literate person could have easily taught brickmakers to write the first letters of their names (*cf.* Alexander 2008, 32).

It should be noted that only a small percentage of marks are ever visible in a building. The symbols could be drawn on any surface of a brick except the bottom surface, which was set against the ground when bricks were left to dry before they were fired (Hiekkanen 2003, 31). As only one side of the brick could be left visible and the top surface was always left unseen in brickwork, this leaves only a 16 percent chance that a mark would be on a visible face of a brick. For the sake of comparison, Alexander has calculated that there is a 20 percent chance that a mason's mark would

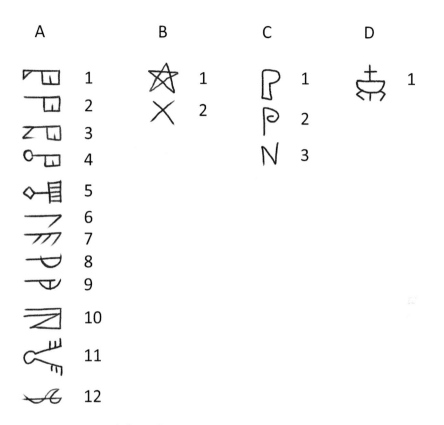

Fig. 2.3: A. Representing symbols B. Abstract symbols C. Letters D. Owner's marks. A1 Turku Cathedral, Lieto Church, Rusko Church and Aboa Vetus & Ars Nova Museum (Turku), A2-3 Rusko Church, A4 Turku Cathedral, A5 Turku Castle, A6-7 Rusko Church, A8-9 Turku Cathedral, A10 Aboa Vetus & Ars Nova Museum (Turku), A11-A12 Turku Cathedral. B1-2 Turku Cathedral, Kuusisto Castle and Aboa Vetus & Ars Nova Museum. C1-3 Turku Cathedral. D1 Kastelholm Castle (Elina Helkala)

be visible in a building (Alexander 2008, 34). The absence or presence of marked bricks could also be explained by different situations: for example, in England masons' marks were used when the work was paid by measure, but they are absent when the wages were paid by the day (Alexander 2008, 29).

Locations of the marks

Medieval bricks with carved marks have been found in Finland in several churches, in castles and in some private houses in Turku. Such marks exist at least in Turku Cathedral (Rinne 1941, 309), Häme Castle (Ratilainen 1997), Kuusisto Castle (Venhe 1994), Kastelholm Castle, Turku Castle, in the churches of Maaria, Katariina (Turku), Lieto, Raisio and Rusko and in medieval houses in Turku, where the marked bricks found in a single house in Aboa Vetus & Ars Nova Museum have been published

(Aalto 2015).The marks seem to be especially common around Turku, which is hardly surprising as this was the administrative, spiritual, and commercial centre of medieval eastern Sweden. For this reason, Turku became also the centre of brick industry in medieval Finland (Kuokkanen 1981, 42). These marks remain unknown from secular contexts in other medieval towns in present-day Finland, which is explained by the fact that Turku was the only town where private masonry buildings were constructed. Other Finnish towns were dominated by log buildings (Seppänen 2014; Niukkanen, Seppänen & Suhonen 2014, 93–94).

There are only a few standing medieval brick buildings in present-day Finland. The most prominent of them are Turku Cathedral, Häme Castle and the Holy Cross Church in Hattula, situated near Häme Castle (Fig. 2.1) (Kuokkanen 1981, 17–18; Svanberg 2013, 13, 29–31). The choir of *Nousis* (Nousiainen) Church, the sacristy of *Storkyro* (Isokyrö) Church and the longhouse of *Kyrkslätt* (Kirkkonummi) Church are also built of brick (Hiekkanen 1994, 166–167; 2007, 120–125, 441, 501). Turku Cathedral (Rinne 1941, 309) and Häme Castle (Ratilainen 1997) have provided an abundance of different brickmakers' marks, but somewhat surprisingly none are known in Hattula Church (Ratilainen 2011, 382–385).

Of all the above-mentioned buildings, Turku Cathedral has the largest collection of different marks visible *in situ* in the brickwork. Although the marks in Turku Cathedral are clearly visible (Figs 2.4 A and B), no thorough analysis of the material has ever been made. Curiously, these marks are concentrated in the most prominent part of

Fig. 2.4 A: All Saints Chapel in Turku Cathedral was built in the late 15th century. Several brickmakers' marks are visible on its outer wall (Author)

Fig. 2.4 B: Marks representing keys are some of the most common seen on the wall of Turku Cathedral's All Saints Chapel (Author)

the building, the medieval All Saints Chapel (present-day High Choir). This octagonal chapel was built in the late 15th century and it is the final medieval addition to the row of side chapels surrounding the cathedral. Rinne (1941, 309) noted the fact that the bricks used in the chapel are of unusually high quality. He deduced that the bricks were clearly manufactured by professional craftsmen, which was, in his opinion, further attested by the fact that these were the only bricks marked with brickmakers' marks.

Who were the brickmakers?

Written sources reveal very little about the artisans who made the bricks or the locations where bricks were produced. Brickyards are known to have existed in Turku and *Viborg* (Viipuri). At least the brickyards on Kakskerta island in Turku and in Papula near Viipuri were owned by Dominican friars, and Dominicans have been believed to have had a considerable impact on the spreading of the craft. To date, only one possibly medieval brickyard in Finland has been studied archaeologically, that at Herniäinen, close to Hattula Church (Kuokkanen 1981, 17–18, 28, 42–46).

One question concerning the brickmakers who worked in the Diocese of Turku is their ethnicity. It has been presumed that the brickmakers were mostly of foreign, probably German, origin (Gardberg 1957, 75; Kuokkanen 1981, 18). Medieval written sources mention foreign brickmakers only in connection with one event. Turku Cathedral was damaged in a fire in 1509 and dean of Turku Paulus Scheel attempted to hire brickmakers from Stralsund and Lübeck to repair it (FMU 5751, FMU 5825, FMU 5827, FMU 5834). The sources also mention two Finnish brickmakers; peculiarly both had the same name, Tiili-Pieti or Brick-Peter (the word 'brick' is *tiili* in Finnish and *tegel* in Swedish). The bailiff of Häme Castle Valdemar Djäkn (mentioned between 1406–1435) reclaimed a field from the older *Tili Peti* (Tiili-Pieti) sometime in the first half of the 15th century (FMU 3437). The younger Tiili-Pieti (called *Tegil Peti, Tegil Per* and *Tigel Per* in the sources) is mentioned five times in connection to assemblies held in Sääksmäki and Saarioinen in southern Finland in years 1507 and 1508 (Suvanto 1995, 176–177). It seems probable that the younger Tiili-Pieti could have been a descendant or some other relative of the older one, as they both lived in the castle fief of Häme Castle. Peter seems to have been a common name amongst the brickmakers, as in mainland Sweden one *Peter tegelslagare* (Peter the brickmaker) was mentioned in 1436 as a recipient of inherited land in Norrbo (SDHK 22653). In 1489 one *Lars Tegelslagare* (Lars Brickmaker) was mentioned in Stockholm as one signatory of a receipt of a monetary transaction (SDHK 32209). People travelled effortlessly between Stockholm and Turku, and it is not impossible that Peter or Lars could have worked in the Diocese of Turku as well.

Although there were also local brickmakers mentioned in the sources, most of the master masons mentioned seem to have been German-speaking craftsmen from Livonia or northern Germany. In 1431, for example, one master mason Simon from Reval (present-day Tallinn) oversaw the rebuilding of the Dominican convent of St Olof in Turku (FMU 1977). In 1477, in connection with the construction of Olavinlinna Castle in Eastern Finland, sixteen *'gode vtlendske muremestere'* (good foreign master masons) are mentioned (FMU 3733). These men were probably Livonian, an idea that gets further support from a later mention from the year 1481, when master mason Oleff Hergk from Reval worked at the same castle (FMU 3880). However, it has even been proposed that they would have been Greek or Italian craftsmen (Gardberg 1957, 16).

At times, the masons seem to have fired the bricks they needed themselves. For example, the bailiff's accounts of Häme Castle mention one Knut the mason who fired 1500 bricks and built stoves in the scribes' quarters and visitors' quarters of the castle in 1541 (Vilkuna 1998, 169; Vilkuna 2003, 69). Some of the brickmakers are also known to have been peasant craftsmen; brickmaking on Kakskerta island in modern

Turku was mentioned in 1556, and the village name *Tiilisali* (Brick hall) hints that the production had probably begun already earlier in the Middle Ages (Oja 1981, 136).

Knowing where the brickmakers came from could help us to understand why brickmakers' marks were in use in the Diocese of Turku but not elsewhere in Sweden. Marking bricks was certainly not only a Finnish phenomenon, as such markings are known already in Roman bricks and in medieval times for example in medieval Flanders (Debonne 2009) and northern Germany (Rümelin 2003). In the light of the few written sources, it would be tempting to assume that the tradition of marking bricks was brought from the southern shore of the Baltic Sea by German brickmakers, but further study is needed to prove this. The custom of stamping bricks is believed to have begun in northern Germany at the end of the 14th century or in the beginning of the 15th century, at latest by the 1420s (Rümelin 2003, 144). It should also be noted that marked bricks already existed in Russia by the end of the 13th century (Antipov & Gervais 2015) and some medieval bricks with brickmakers' marks have also been documented in Livonia (Ose 2015, 76–77). It is also quite possible that the tradition could have spread from either Russia or Livonia.

The Finnish marks differ from the German marks in two aspects. Firstly, the German marks were made with stamps while the Finnish marks were drawn by hand. Secondly, the symbols used in the marks are distinctly different. Thus, it does not seem that the tradition of marking bricks would have been a straightforward cultural loan, although the origin of the idea could have been in the German brickmakers' stamps. If this was the case, the reason for using hand drawn marks instead of stamps could be explained by different levels of organization. The German brickyards were mostly permanent institutions (Rümelin 2003), whereas in the Diocese of Turku, temporary brickyards were set up when needed (Kuokkanen 1981, 42–46). The stamping of bricks seems to have begun in Sweden only in the 18th century, in tandem with establishing more permanent and organized brickyards (Kuokkanen 1981, 114–178; Meissner 2010, 35).

Function of the marks

Brickmakers' marks were probably made for the same reason as stonecutters marked stones with masons' marks – to sign the production and to get paid for the done work (Alexander 2007, 64–65 2008, 29; Ose 2015, 76–77). Such masons' marks exist also in the medieval stone churches in Sweden (Gardelin 2006, 62), but not in the Diocese of Turku. The reason is that in Finland the stone building tradition differed somewhat from that in mainland Sweden. Limestone deposits in Finland are very limited and masonry buildings were mostly built of unworked or only roughly shaped natural blocks of plutonic rocks instead of easily worked limestone. The churches were also whitewashed, which meant that the stones used in construction did not need to be completely even (Hiekkanen 2003, 33). The unworked stone surfaces would have been ill-suited for engraving signs.

Finnish brickmakers' marks relate mostly to everyday life. They represent household items that could have been found in almost every late medieval home. At the same time, there is more to the symbols than meets the eye, all these household items are also attributes of Roman Catholic saints. Keys are the attribute of St Peter, the axe of St Olof, the halberdier of St Matthew, the gridiron of St Lawrence, and St Andrew's cross is obviously that of St Andrew. Anchors are mentioned by Lindberg (1919, 31) in the church of Lieto nearby Turku and are the attribute of St Clement (Farmer 2011, section on Clement). This is hardly a coincidence. Saints were strongly present in the everyday lives of medieval people and their attributes would have been easily recognizable for all. Such symbols spread widely in Europe in the 13th century (Edgrén 2000, 87).

By the 15th century, almost all Finns were given name after saints (Salminen 2013, 379). Considering this, it would seem plausible that the brickmakers' marks did not refer only to the saints, but also to brickmakers themselves. In an illiterate culture, these symbols could easily have served as personal signatures, as a person living in the Middle Ages would have instantly associated the attributes with saints and their names. Thus, a medieval person would, for example, have thought of St Olof when he saw a symbol representing an axe (Aalto 2015, 7–8). In this way attributes of saints would have been generally better understood than letters, which could have been read only by a limited group of literate people. The idea is supported by the fact that the saints represented in brickmakers' marks were all popular namesakes in late medieval Finland; for example, in the church parish of Helsinga in *Nyland* (Uusimaa), Per (Peter), Olof, Lars (Lawrence), Mats (Matthew), Anders (Andrew) and Clemet were in the fifteen most common names given to males in the early 16th century (Salminen 2013, 383).

Referring to the name of an individual via the attributes or even pictures of saints was certainly a custom in another medieval medium of personal identification, i.e. personal seals. Reinhold Hausen (1900) has catalogued a total of 364 Finnish medieval seals that have survived either attached to medieval documents or as the original seal matrices. Pictures of saints or attributes of saints are in some cases used as the motif of personal seals or coat of arms. This practice seems to have been more common among the clergy, but it was not unknown amongst the laity either. Aside from episcopal seals where it became customary to depict the first bishop of Finland, St Henry, saints or their attributes are used at least in 13 cases (Hausen 1900, nos. 37, 40, 43, 44, 47, 48, 49, 56, 57, 61, 63, 67 and 72). Amongst the nobility attributes of saints were used at least in three instances (Hausen 1900, nos. 177, 333 and 334).

In most of these cases, the saint depicted in the seal was the eponym of the seal's owner. For example, a squire called Anders Jakobsson had St Andrew's cross in his seal (Hausen 1900, no. 333). Amongst the priestly seals, it seems to have been common to depict the whole saint; for example, dean (later bishop of Turku) Lars Suurpää had St Lawrence depicted in his seal (Hausen 1900, no. 37), dean Paulus Scheel had the picture of St Paul (Hausen 1900, no. 38) and both priest Matts Oloffsson (Hausen 1900, no. 49) and vicar Matts Larsson (Hausen 1900, no. 67) had the picture of St Matthew in their seals. It could well be that the brickmakers' marks functioned in the same way, being both representations of the brickmaker's given name and perhaps even a form of prayer or a devotional image to the artisan's divine intercessor.

The visual world of the signs

Brickmakers' marks did not exist as an isolated form of art. They resemble attributes of saints depicted as line drawings in wooden calendar staves known as rune staves. The marks also have a strong resemblance to the so-called builder paintings (also earlier primitive paintings), simple church paintings executed in red ochre.

Late medieval rune staves were wooden calendars inscribed with runes marking the days of the week. Important ecclesial dates were marked on the staves with symbols that could be either the attribute of the saint remembered on that day or a symbol of an agrarian chore that should have been done on the specific day (Fig. 2.5). The rune staves were introduced in southern Scandinavia in the beginning of the 11th century, and they remained in use to the 19th century (Oja 2015, 81). In the late Middle Ages, the people living in Scandinavia and Finland were very familiar with rune staves – Swedish bishop and historian Olaus Magnus even tells in his book *Historia de gentibus septentrionalibus* that it was common to use them as walking sticks to keep track of the time while travelling (Magnus 2010 [1555], 732). It is uncertain if the medieval brickmakers were familiar with these wooden calendars, but considering their popularity in the 16th century, it seems likely. In any case, the tradition of marking the feast days of saints with the saints' attributes reveals that the symbols were commonly used by themselves to refer to the saint in question. This suggests there could have been a connection between the brickmakers' marks and the marks in rune staves.

Builder paintings found in Finnish late medieval churches depict religious motifs, coats of arms and fables. Such paintings exist in 47 stone churches in the medieval Diocese of Turku (Fält 2012). It should be noted that, similarly to the brickmakers' marks, the builders' paintings are also a phenomenon that is present in the Diocese of Turku, but not elsewhere in Sweden (Fält 2012, 15). It seems evident that these paintings and brickmakers' marks are part of the same visual culture. For example, the gridiron symbol in Turku Castle looks remarkably like the gridiron held by St

Fig. 2.5: The feast days of saints were marked in rune staves with the corresponding saint's attribute. In some staves the symbols bear striking resemblance to brickmakers' marks. This 16th century staff is from Denmark. The figure is drawn after a photograph published in Lebech 1969 (Elina Helkala)

Fig. 2.6 A: St Lawrence depicted with his attribute gridiron on the wall of Maaria Church (Turku). These so-called builder paintings can be seen belonging to the same visual world as brickmakers' marks (Elina Helkala)

Fig. 2.6 B: The gridiron mark in Turku Castle bears striking resemblance to the way the item is depicted in builder paintings (Author)

Lawrence painted in the Church of Maaria in Turku (Figs 2.6 A and B; the location of Maaria Church is shown in Fig. 2.2). Although the style of brickmakers' marks and builder paintings seems very similar, there is still a caveat: one could argue that there are not many ways to depict an item in a line drawing.

It is very likely that church painters and brickmakers were familiar with each other's works, as they were probably members of the same building teams. It is also interesting to note that the timeframe for the brickmakers' marks and builder paintings seems to be roughly the same: builder paintings were produced between 1430–1540 (Fält 2012, 14) and the marks can be dated to the same period (Aalto 2015, 5–7). The connection could, however, be explained by the fact that this period was a time of relatively intensive church building in Finland.

Conclusion

It is probable that Finnish brickmakers' marks were used in much the same manner as masons' marks elsewhere in Europe – to identify the artisan, perhaps in order to pay his wages. The limited distribution of the key symbol discussed in this paper suggests that the symbols could indeed have been personal. There is much uncertainty about the origin of the tradition in Finland, and the situation is further confused by the fact that the marks were not used in mainland Sweden. The tradition could have spread to Finland either from Livonia, Russia or German areas of the Baltic Sea. Regardless of the origin of the tradition, it seems to have begun in the Diocese of Turku during the 15th century and continued at least to the first quarter of the 16th century, lasting for several generations of brickmakers.

The symbols used as brickmakers' marks are part of medieval visual culture. The images are related to medieval builder paintings in Finnish churches and attributes of saints depicted in rune staves. It seems plausible that many of the marks depicting household items are actually referring to Catholic saints as a way of expressing brickmakers' identity. This would have been natural in a society where only a few could read, but where the attributes of saints were instantly recognizable for anyone. If this is correct, the brickmakers' marks could reveal the names and working areas of several medieval individuals who are otherwise lost to history.

Acknowledgements

I would like to express my gratitude to Tanja Ratilainen (Turku Museum Centre) for commenting on the draft and Johannes Suoranta for checking the language of this paper. I thank also my wife Elina Helkala for providing the illustrations for this article.

Bibliography

Aalto, I. (2015) Avain, kirves, risti ja tähti – tiilentekijöiden merkkejä keskiajan Turusta. *Suomen Keskiajan Arkeologian Seura* 3–4/2014, 3–10.
Alexander, J. S. (2007) The introduction and use of masons' marks in Romanesque buildings in England. *Medieval Archaeology* 51, 63–81.

Alexander, J. S. (2008) Masons' marks and the working practices of medieval masons. In P. S. Barnell & A. Pacey (eds.) *Who built Beverley Minister?* 21–40. Reading, Spire Books Ltd.

Antipov, I. & Gervais, A. (2015) The bricks from St. Nicholas Church at Lipno near Novgorod (1292) and the origins of the new Novgorodian building tradition. *Estonian Journal of Archaeology* 1/2015, 58–79.

Bernotas, R. (2013) Brick-making in medieval Livonia – the Estonian example. *Estonian Journal of Archaeology* 2/2013, 139–156.

Bernotas, R. (2017) *New aspects of the genesis of the medieval town walls in the Northern Baltic Sea region.* Ph.D. thesis, Archaeology. Turku, University of Turku.

Debonne, V. (2009) Production of moulded bricks on a Gothic building site. The case of the thirteenth-century abbeys of The Dunes and Boudelo (Belgium). In K.-E. Kurrer, W. Lorenz, & V. Wetzk (eds.) *Proceedings of the Third International Congress on Construction History* (Brandenburg University of Technology Cottbus, Germany, 20th–24th May 2009), 459–464. Cottbus, Brandenburg University of Technology.

Edgrén, H. (2000) Taiteen merkitys keskiajan kirkossa. In M.-L. Linder, M.-R. Saloniemi & C. Krötzl (eds.) *Ristin ja Olavin kansaa. Keskiajan usko ja kirkko Hämeessä ja Satakunnassa*, 85–89. Tampere, Tampereen museot.

Ekko, P. O. (1984) *Puumerkit ja riimut menneisyyden avaimina.* Helsinki, Suomen heraldinen seura.

Ekko, P. O. (2008) *Länsi-Suomen puumerkkejä seuraavista pitäjistä: Raisio.* http://www.oh1sa.net/data/mirrors/OH1SM_Timo/puumerkki/LSUOMIPU.htm#RAISIO [Accessed 19.05.2017].

Farmer, D. (2011) *The Oxford Dictionary of Saints.* 5th revised edition. Oxford, Oxford University Press.

Fält, K. (2012) *Wall Paintings, Workshops and Visual Production in the Medieval Diocese of Turku from 1430 to 1540.* Suomen Muinaismuistoyhdistyksen aikakauskirja 120. Helsinki, Suomen Muinaismuistoyhdistys.

Gardberg, C. J. (1957) *Med murslev och timmerbila. Drag ur det finländska byggnadshantverkets historia.* Med byggare i 800 år. Helsinki, Unknown Publisher.

Gardelin, G. (2006) *En värld av sten. Stenhuggarnas organisation i medeltidens Östergötland.* Lund, Lunds universitet.

Haggrén, G. (2015) Keskiajan arkeologia. In G. Haggrén *et al.* (eds.) *Muinaisuutemme jäljet. Suomen esi- ja varhaishistoria kivikaudelta keskiajalle*, 367–535. Helsinki, Gaudeamus.

Harjula, J. (2008) Arkeologia ja muuttuva keskiajan kirjallisen kulttuurin kuva. *Kasvatus & Aika* 3 (2)/2008, 7–25. Helsinki, Suomen kasvatuksen ja koulutuksen historian seura.

Hausen, R. (ed.) (1900) *Finlands medeltidssigill.* Helsinki, Finlands Statsarkiv.

Hausen, R. (ed.) (1910–1935) *Finlands medeltidsurkunder* I–VIII (FMU) (1910–1935). Helsinki, Finlands Statsarkiv.

Hiekkanen, M. (1994) *The Stone Churches of the Medieval Diocese of Turku. A Systematic Classification and Chronology.* Suomen Muinaismuistoyhdistyksen aikakauskirja 101. Helsinki, Suomen Muinaismuistoyhdistys.

Hiekkanen, M. (2000) A Brick Carving in the So-Called Chapel of Hämeenlinna Castle. In K. Alttoa, K. Drake, K. Pospieszny and K. Uotila (eds.) *Castella Maris Baltici* 3–4, 217–219. Turku, Tarto and Malbork, The Society for Medieval Archaeology in Finland.

Hiekkanen, M. (2003) *Suomen kivikirkot keskiajalla.* Helsinki, Otava.

Hiekkanen, M. (2007) *Suomen keskiajan kivikirkot.* Helsinki, Suomalaisen Kirjallisuuden Seura.

Kuokkanen, R. (1981) *Suomen tiiliteollisuuden historia. Osa I: Tiilen lyönti ja käyttö ristiretkiajalta 1850-luvulle.* Helsinki, Suomen tiiliteollisuusliitto ry and Tiilikeskus Oy.

Lebech, M. (1969) *Fra runestav till almanak.* København, Thejls.

Lindberg, C. (1919) *Om teglets användning i finska medeltida gråstenskyrkor.* Helsingfors, Unknown publisher.

Magnus, O. (2010 [1555]) *Historia om de nordiska folken.* Möklinta, Gidlunds förlag.

Meissner, K. (2010) *Stämplade tegel i Kalmar län.* Kalmar, Kalmar läns museum.

Niukkanen, M., Seppänen, L. & Suhonen, M. (2014) Kaupunkirakentaminen Suomessa keskiajalla. In H. Lilius & P. Kärki (eds.) *Suomen kaupunkirakentamisen historia* I, 27–94. Helsinki, Suomalaisen Kirjallisuuden Seura.

Oja, A. (1981) Kaarina keskiajalla ja 1500-luvulla. In *Kaarinan pitäjän historia* I, 37–308. Turku, Kaarinan historiatoimikunta.

Oja, H. (2015) *Riimut. Viestejä viikingeiltä.* Helsinki, Suomalaisen Kirjallisuuden Seura.

Ose, I. (2015) *Building ceramics of Turaida castle in the 13th-17th centuries. Catalogue.* Turaida, Turaida Museum Reserve.

Ratilainen, T. (1997) *Hämeen linnan tiilissä esiintyvät jäljet ja piirrokset – ja pohdintaa niiden synnystä ja tarkoituksesta.* Unpublished pro seminar paper, Archaeology, University of Turku.

Ratilainen, T. (2011) Kilroy was here: A glimpse of the graffiti of Holy Cross Church in Hattula. In J. Harjula, M. Helamaa & J. Haarala (eds.) *Times, Things and Places. 36 Essays for Jussi-Pekka Taavitsainen*, 380–391. Turku, J.-P. Taavitsainen Festschrift Committee.

Ratilainen, T. (2012) *Tiiliä tulkitsemassa. Hattulan Pyhän Ristin kirkon muuraaminen keskiajalla.* Licentiate thesis, Archaeology. Turku, University of Turku.

Ratilainen, T. (2014) Unfired bricks used for a medieval oven in Turku, Finland. In T. Ratilainen, R. Bernotas & C. Herrmann (eds.) *Fresh Approaches to Brick Production and Use in the Middle Ages. Proceedings of the session 'Utilization of Brick in the Medieval Period – Production, Construction, Destruction' Held at the European Association of Archaeologists (EAA) Meeting, 29 August to 1 September 2012 in Helsinki, Finland.* British Archaeological Reports International Series 2611, 93–101. Oxford, Publishers for British Archaeological Reports.

Ratilainen, T. (2016) At the dawn of masonry architecture – church remains and associated brick structures at Koroinen, Turku. *Estonian Journal of Archaeology* 1/2016, 54–80.

Ratilainen, T. (2017) Lyhyt kommentti Ilari Aallon artikkelissa esiintyneeseen väärinkäsitykseen tiilentekijöiden merkkien merkityksestä tiilitutkimukselle. *Suomen Keskiajan Arkeologian Seura* 2/2016, 46–47.

Rinne, J. (1941) *Turun tuomiokirkko keskiaikana* I. *Turun tuomiokirkon rakennushistoria.* Turku, Turun tuomiokirkon isännistö.

Rümelin, H. (2003) Ziegelstempel. Zur bedeutung eines spätmittelalterlichen details der Baustoffproduktion in der Altmark. In E. Badstübner & D. Schumann (eds.) *Backsteintechnologien in Mittelalter und Neuzeit. Studien zur Backsteinarchitektur*, 129–177. Berlin, Lukas Verlag.

Salminen, T. (2013) *Vantaan ja Helsingin pitäjän keskiaika.* Vantaa, Vantaan kaupunki.

Seppänen, L. (2012) *Rakentaminen ja kaupunkikuvan muutokset keskiajan Turussa. Erityistarkastelussa Åbo Akademin päärakennuksentontin arkeologinen aineisto.* Ph.D. thesis, Archaeology, University of Turku.

Seppänen, L. (2014) Brick buildings, chimneys, and windows with glass: A chain of changes in medieval housing in Turku. *Finskt museum* 2012, 6–27. Helsinki, Finska fornminnesföreningen.

Suvanto, S. (1995) *Yksilö myöhäiskeskiajan talonpoikaisyhteiskunnassa. Sääksmäen kihlakunta 1400-luvun alusta 1570-luvulle.* Helsinki, Suomen Historiallinen Seura.

Svanberg, J. (2013) *Medeltida byggmästare i Norden.* Stockholm, Bokförlaget Signum.

Svenskt Diplomatariums huvudkartotek (SDHK). Riksarkivet. https://sok.riksarkivet.se/sdhk [Accessed 19.5.2017]

Uotila, K. (2003) Kivitaloja keskiajan Turussa. In L. Seppänen (ed.) *Kaupunkia pintaa syvemmältä. Arkeologisia näkökulmia Turun historiaan.* Archaeologia Medii Aevi Finlandiae IX, 121–134. Turku, The Society for Medieval Archaeology in Finland.

Uotila, K. (2007) Aboa Vetus -museon kivirakennusten tutkimukset v. 2002–2006. *Suomen Keskiajan Arkeologian Seura* 2/2007, 18–27.

Uotila, K. (2009) Keskiajan arkeologia. In M. Lamberg, A. Lahtinen & S. Niiranen (eds.) *Keskiajan avain*, 300–318. Helsinki, Suomalaisen Kirjallisuuden Seura.

Venhe, L. (1994) Irtaimet tiililöydöt. In A. Suna (ed.) *Kuusiston linna. Tutkimuksia 1985-1993.* Museoviraston rakennushistorian osaston raportteja 8, 32–39. Helsinki, Museovirasto.

Vilkuna, A.-M. (1998) *Kruunun taloudenpito Hämeen linnassa 1500-luvun puolivälissä.* Bibliotheca Historica 31. Helsinki, Suomen Historiallinen Seura.

Vilkuna, A.-M. (2003) Financial management at Häme Castle in the mid-sixteenth century (1539 – about 1570). In T. Mikkola and A.-M. Vilkuna (eds.) *At Home within Stone Walls: Life in the Late Medieval Häme Castle.* Archaeologia Medii Aevi Finlandiae VIII, 15–132. Turku, The Society for Medieval Archaeology in Finland.

Chapter 3

The medieval and early post-medieval weighing houses at Gammel Strand, Copenhagen, Denmark

Stuart Whatley

Introduction

Archaeological excavations and recent research have suggested that the harbourside of Copenhagen developed to provide a profitable harbour for shipping and trade. The need for a deeper harbour due to advancements in shipbuilding technology led to the constant creation of new land in the south of the city and the urbanisation of the surrounding area. By the 1400s, the harbourside had expanded southwards and was centralised in the area that would be later known as *Gammel Strand* (Old Beach), which obtained a new set of public administrative buildings focussed on trade. This new public harbour area was subsequently surrounded at the north, east and west by private housing for the elites, and guarded to the south by the royal castle. The area developed into a zone comprising a curious mix of maritime industry, administration, elite private housing and the base of the fishing industry, existing side by side in a way that would not occur in modern times. The weighing house buildings were located on the southern border of Copenhagen, and maritime border to the Baltic Sea and the North Sea (Whatley *et al.* 2016, 2–3).

The information for this research comes primarily from the Metro Cityring excavations, undertaken by the Museum of Copenhagen from 2009–2017. The project comprised a total of 17 investigations at locations for new stations surrounding the inner city, with the most important excavations located on the former medieval boundaries of Copenhagen at *Rådhuspladsen* (Town hall square) and *Kongens Nytorv* (Kings square) (the site of the *Vesterport* (western gate) and *Østerport* (eastern gate) respectively) and on Gammel Strand, the former harbourside (Figs 3.1 and 3.2). This new information will be supplemented by earlier excavations and historical records within the city.

Fig. 3.1: Close detail from the 1840 daguerreotype photo of Gammel Strand, depicting the weighing house of 1581, located centre-left (Museum of Copenhagen)

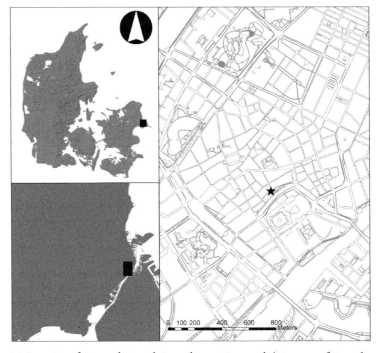

Fig. 3.2: Location of Gammel Strand, Copenhagen, Denmark (Museum of Copenhagen)

Weighing houses, origin, function & location

This article will focus on the weighing houses from the Late Medieval and early post-medieval periods recorded as being located at Gammel Strand. These buildings were essential for taxing goods imported into Copenhagen, and their location on the harbourside provided easy access into the town marketplace via the waterways. Ayers (2016, 164) writes that weighing houses (in general) served the usual functions of both providing a public check on goods and enabling the imposition of appropriate taxes; where goods were brought in to be weighed and taxed before offloading to the markets. Dijkman (2011, 210–214) states that these buildings were either administered by city officials or by officials appointed by lords or the crown, depending on the country of origin and whether the weighing house was situated in an urban or rural area. Dijkman (2011, 224) has also noted that the ownership of weighing houses may have changed over time; as until 1320 in England, weighing houses were the responsibility of the crown, with urban officials and town governments later assuming control. Although some weighing houses were small rural buildings, others in cities were large, ostentatious structures and could arguably be seen as a visual public symbol of the city, as in Copenhagen.

The use of a weighing house portrays the development of harbours and changes in how trade was conducted in the medieval period. As Milne argues with his harbour development hypothesis, the construction of a tax building represents one of the constituents of the new merchant-type harbour (Milne 1999, 147). He argues merchant harbours developed from the beach-type harbour of the period 800s–1200s, which involved more of a barter economy, undertaken on shorelines and beaches. Trade was undertaken between craftspeople selling their goods, where warehouses in the form of huts, and storage buildings and pits were created for seasonal trading. This all changed with the growth of the monetary economy in the high medieval period, which in turn led to merchants becoming middlemen between the craftsmen. With the developments in ship design from flat-bottomed vessels to hull type vessels, the harbours required a pier or bulwark so ships could dock and offload goods. Buildings involved with tax were either constructed or made available for use in towns, and officials were placed in charge of weighing and taxing for the rulers or magistrates of the city. Warehouses then became necessary to store trade goods awaiting taxation or transport (Milne 1999, 147).

Weighing houses were common in northwestern Europe and the Baltic Sea region and were especially prevalent in Hanseatic League ports (Ayers 2016, 103). They appear from the 1300s with examples such as Hull in 1365 (Ayers 2016, 163), Krakow in 1300 (Wardas-Lason & Garbacz-Klempka 2016, 62), only ending when weights and measures became internationally organised rather than based on a city and nation standard. Similar types of buildings existed, but under another name as customs houses or as toll houses, as in Bruges with the *Tolhuis* (Ayers 2016, 163), which may have amalgamated many roles which were separated in Copenhagen with a toll house and weighing house. It is unclear if customs houses contained the town weight, but they appear to have held administration roles similar to weighing houses, and the Early Post medieval weighing house in Copenhagen was both a custom and a weighing house in the 1600s (Whatley et al, 2016, 154) Examples of cities containing customs houses include London, Paris, Venice and Bristol. The London customs house was founded in 1377 by John Churchman, originally for taxing wool. As in Copenhagen, it was replaced in the mid-1500s by a much sturdier and larger building (Milne 2006, 122–124).

Weighing houses in Copenhagen

The first recorded mention of a weighing house in Copenhagen dates to 1281. In a letter by the Bishop of Roskilde, then Lord of Copenhagen, the *Fogeden* (Copenhagen Bailiffs), were given the authority to establish institutions to benefit the town and its inhabitants, this included reference to a weighing house. This building would be involved with weighing, controlling and price assessment of goods, with special reference to the measurement of German beer 'as this had been sold inaccurately resulting in loss for the buyers and destruction of the salesmen's souls' (Nielsen 1872, 27, 29–30; 1877b, 69; Whatley *et al.* 2016, 31). It is not known whether a weighing house was built, as one is not mentioned again until the 1400s, but it is probable that taxing of trade goods would have occurred either in a high medieval weighing house or in a public building near the harbour.

The next mention of a weighing house is in the town privileges of 1443 (Nielsen 1872, 127: 57), where King Christoffer of Bavaria cited the need for a weighing house. It is unsure if this suggests a replacement building or that one should be built, but as public weighing houses have been constructed in reciprocal trading ports from the late 1300s, it is expected that Copenhagen should have had a similar type structure.

From at least the early 1500s a weighing house was most likely in existence and Nielsen stated that the old weight house was situated between present-day Kompagninstræde and Snaregade (Nielsen 1877a, 85), he later changed it to being situated the southern side of Snaregade, on the corner of the road Naboløs (Nielsen 1881, 152; 1872, 217: 304, 276: 397, 282: 402, 297: 425; 1879a, 330: 336). Perhaps Nielsen had made a mistake when writing in 1877 on the location of the weighing house, which he changed later in 1881, or perhaps the sources which he interpreted may have recorded dates of the previous weighing house to the Late Medieval weighing house at the bottom of Snaregade on Gammel Strand (Whatley *et al.* 2016, 30). It is this location that may represent the foundations of the Late Medieval weighing house discussed in this article

The Late Medieval weighing house of Copenhagen

The Late Medieval weighing house was identified from the 2010 phase of the Gammel Strand excavations. Although not completely uncovered due to the trench dimensions, the building spanned an area measuring 4 × 4 m, and is expected to be at least twice the size (Fig. 3.3). It was located in an area 25 m north of the modern-day canal, 20 m south of the extant Gammel Strand buildings and 10 m east of the Nybrogade

Fig. 3.3: Brick and stone sub-base uncovered beneath the eastern wall of the possible Late Medieval Weighing House (Museum of Copenhagen)

building no. 2, beneath the modern-day square on Gammel Strand. This location is very similar to that of the recorded *vejerhus (weighing house)* from the 1500s (Nielsen 1881, 152). The excavated building was constructed upon land reclamation deposits, but due to the inherent instability of the newly created land, posts and planks were used to form a wooden bulwark-type foundation to stabilise the new structure. The 2 m long posts were sturdy and pushed into the natural ground. Further stability was provided through a brick and stone foundation, although a buttress-type wall was also added in one place, which may have been another type of foundation.

The overlying weighing house building was, as with the weighing houses from Hull, Amsterdam, Bremen, Gdansk, and Stockholm (Evans 1997, 35–49), fashioned from brick. The structure comprised two rooms; a northern room comprising the remains of a wooden floor, and a southern room comprising only the remaining cellar. This building has recently been reinterpreted after formerly being depicted as a building with one room and a southern extension with a cellar as recorded in the Gammel

Strand excavation reports by Olesen and Bork-Pedersen (2012, 138–146) and Whatley *et al.* (2016, 81–86).

The possible *vejerhus* was set on a NNW–SSE orientation. The remains were heavily truncated, as the stones had been robbed. Good building stone and bricks were likely to have been re-used which may explain the extreme level of robbing, as stone is scarce in Denmark. The area also truncated by many service trenches interred from the late 1800s onwards. Some of these trenches were observed by archaeologists, with Rosenkjær (1902) and Smidt (1902) both observing archaeological remains in the area. Rosenkjær recorded that there was a timber-built slipway resting on a wooden bulwark, which was probably the wooden floor from the Late Medieval weighing house (Whatley *et al.* 2016, 31–33, 87).

The main walls of the structure were only partially uncovered due to the trench positioning, with only the eastern side represented. This comprised of a fragment of wall overlying a foundation sub-base which formed the eastern wall of the building. The wall is expected to have been approximately 1.15 m in width, loadbearing and wide enough to carry a second storey. The eastern wall foundation sub-base which overlay the wooden bulwark and stone 'buttress' contained a fragment of Siegburg ware of a form in use from 1300–1500, providing a relative date for the construction. Internally was a single room which consisted of a few layers of a wooden floor (Fig. 3.4), but due to the restrictions of the trench, no corresponding walls were seen. The wooden floor did not contain finds, so was kept clean when in use, and was also seen to have been refurbished and replaced, as there were many layers of wood. This may be due to the damp conditions of the tidal impact on the newly reclaimed land. The extra foundations beneath the eastern wall are now more understandable as it appears, as with excavations behind the 20th-century wall, the effect of the water table and the tides were high at this location. The presence of a wooden floor in a building represents status as they were generally uncommon in this period. Studies from Hull show that common floor styles in this period were simply clay or comprised of a clay platform with

Fig. 3.4: Truncated wooden floor within Room 1 of the Late Medieval weighing house, looking north-west (Museum of Copenhagen)

Fig. 3.5: Cellar from Room 2 of the Late Medieval Weighing house G389, looking north-east (Museum of Copenhagen)

a mortar skin (comprising mortar, broken CBM). Wooden floors only became more common in the 1500s and were for the elites before that date (Evans 1997, 41).

The second room of the structure consisted of a cellar (Fig. 3.5). It was built abutting the eastern wall of the building with the northern wall acting as a partition wall in the building. Although the walls were sturdy they were fashioned from a mixture of brick mortar and various types of stone. The cellar too had flooding problems, as a barrel built into the cellar floor in the northeastern corner of the room was presumably used for drainage. The rest of the cellar floor was generally kept clean, as only a barrel tap was found within. The cellar room probably acted as a storage room as there were very few finds. These were mainly seen within the section of the construction cut for the barrel where Siegburg ware (Fig 3.6), ceramic building material, slag and animal bones were discovered.

The end of the Late Medieval weighing house is not clear, but it was probably linked to size and productivity. The increase in loading docks in the vicinity on Skarnholmene (two small islands in between Gammel Strand and Slotsholmen) in 1549, and another by the old *Toldbod* (Toll-booth) in 1557, on Slotsholmen (for both sites see Fig. 3.7) (Fabricius 1999, 232) would have led to extra trade into the harbour, possibly adding an extra strain on the facilities. This, coupled with the fact that the old weight house was in a poor condition, led to a complaint being sent to the king by the citizens in 1580 on the state of weighing house (Nielsen 1874, 496: 393–396). The king replied

Fig. 3.6: Decorated vessel from Siegburg portraying the arms of Queen Elizabeth 1st. Found within the cellar of the Late Medieval weighing house (Museum of Copenhagen)

with a document in April 1581 from Fredrik II's *Stadsret* (privileges), 'that the mayors and the town council at their expense would rebuild the weighing house and the town and the citizens would not be troubled with this' (Nielsen 1874, 502: 406). The king produced a further document in December 1581 stating that the Mayors would be exempted of *siisefrij* (taxation) of 100 *læster* (a number of barrels) of Rostocker beer while the rebuilding and mending of the weight house was undertaken (Nielsen 1874, 507: 413).

The end of the Late Medieval weighing house is not so clear. Some sources state that the weighing house area is listed as *humlegården* (hop farm) in the 1600s and continued next to the new early post-medieval weighing house (Nielsen 1881, 152). During the excavation, the upper demolition layers of the structure contained finds dating from the period between 1600 and 1650 so there is some activity in the area, but without full excavation it is all speculation of what actually occurred. If the former Late Medieval weighing house building continued for a while it was not in the previous role of weighing house, as this now was transferred in the new early post-medieval building built a few metres directly east (Whatley *et al.* 2016, 90–93).

The early post-medieval weighing house of Copenhagen

The document 'Christopher Valkendorf credits of the town' (Nielsen 1872, 363: 540–542) states that in 1581, Valkendorf let the beautiful weight house be built on (or into) the beach, 'where no one would have thought a house would ever be built', perhaps in the location of the former public toilet of *Hyskenstræde* (Whatley *et al.* 2016, 90–93). This building was located 3 m east of the Late Medieval weighing house, and would probably have continued further south by a few metres.

The 2010 excavation exposed the foundations of this building, which could then be compared with maps and photographs as it was in existence until 1859. It may have first appeared on the oldest map of Copenhagen, where although not labelled, was possibly indicated as a square building on its own abutted to a street and depicted south of Naboløs (see Fig. 3.9). It was later seen in Resen's map of 1674 (Fig. 3.8) where the plot V relates to *die Waage und die neue Fleich-Buden* (the weight and the new slaughter booths) (Fig. 3.11) (Whatley *et al.* 2016, 26).

The early post-medieval weighing house appeared stronger and better constructed than its predecessor. The 2010 excavation uncovered the northern elements of the

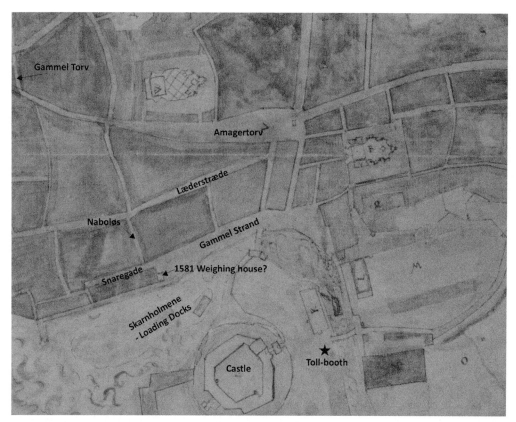

Fig. 3.7: Section of the earliest map of Copenhagen (cropped and turned) showing the Gammel Strand area. North is located to the top of the map, c. 1590s (The Royal Library)

structure showing that it had large stone foundations upon which long *munkesten* (monk type bricks) red brick walls were built. The whole building was found to be approximately 13 m wide and is projected to be up to 18 m long (using measurements linked to the suspected former harbour location in the *vejerhus* area and archaeological remains).

The building was constructed upon bulwarks and posts which were pushed through layers of material laid down to raise and stabilise the ground. Above the posts were the western, eastern and northern foundation walls with an outhouse built on the northwest corner. The wall foundations were 2.2 m wide, to support a building of three floors and a roof with two levels. Various brick construction types were employed on the stone foundations comprising different sized bricks, so it was clear that this area was not meant to be visible to the public. The style changed again when the bases of the lower windows were constructed, which would have been visible on the road. No evidence for the internal layout was revealed apart from some levelling layers. From the observed area, no evidence of cellaring could

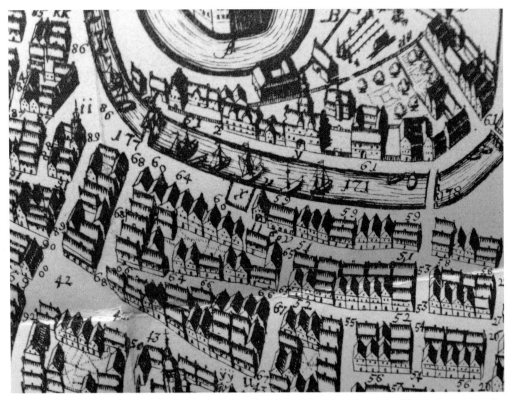

Fig. 3.8: Resens Map of Copenhagen, 1674. Weighing house and slaughter house buildings depicted by the letter V (vejerhus), with the weighing house actually the building to the left. North is at the bottom of the map (The Royal Library)

be seen, but this may still exist in the central and southern part of the building. The lean-to/outhouse, located on the northwestern side of the building was not fully uncovered and was probably a former shed or booth. Due to demolition, the majority of the remains were removed.

Knowledge of how the building would have been used in the early post-medieval period has yet to be found, but it is presumed that the ground floor would have held the town weight. There would have been an office for the town weights master who was in charge of the building, and perhaps rooms for staff (Olesen & Bork-Pedersen 2012, 119–120). All three floors were accessible by large wooden doors or windows seen on the two visible sides of the 1840s daguerreotype photo (Fig. 3.1) and were probably operated via winches as no visible cranes are seen on plans or mentioned in records. It is presumed the middle and southern foundations are preserved under the stone clad square and the road (Whatley *et al.* 2016, 130; fig. 3.10).

Location of weighing houses at Gammel Strand

The role of the weighing house was to tax and weigh goods for the city, so the weighing house had to be located by good transport routes, via rivers, bridges or

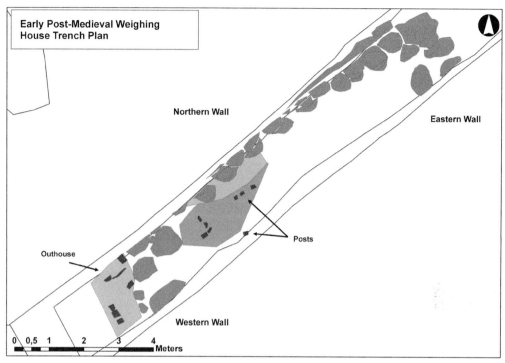

Fig. 3.9: Plan of the possible early post-medieval weighing house (Museum of Copenhagen)

Fig. 3.10: Internal view of the northern foundation wall of the post-medieval weighing house. Indication of a window frame in the upper left corner of the photo (Museum of Copenhagen)

roads. Therefore, their accessibility was crucial for the town to make the process as economically viable as possible. Weighing houses and customs houses appear to be located in areas of space to allow unpacking goods and temporary storage, e.g. Krakow weighing house on the main square (Kowalski 2016, 83), Amsterdam (from 1200s–1600s) on Dam square before moving to the city gate of Sint Antoniespoort (De Graauw 2011, 117–124), or the weighing house at Stockholm in *Jarntorget* (the iron square) (Söderlund 1999, 506–507). The Medieval Customs House at Bristol was located in an area labelled The Triangle with a public area that led towards the main quay (Neale 2000, 87).

Customs and weighing houses were often located on main roads in cities as shown by the still existent *stadtwaage* (weighing house) in Bremen, or on roads leading to the harbour, as with the existing 1600s *Dee Waag* building in Leiden. Other main locations were on riversides, as with London Customs House at Wool quay (Milne 2006, 124) and in Gdansk where the *duza waga miejska* (great city scales) were located by the great crane next to the fortification of the Koga gate (Paner 1999, 398). The weighing houses of Copenhagen, like the London Customs Houses, were located near fortifications which added protection to the economic building. *Slotsholmen* (Castle Island) was located directly south of Gammel Strand protecting the harbour, as Customs House in London was located near the Tower of London (Milne 2006, 119). Although it may be coincidental why they were located next to defensive sites, they also benefited from the protection. The harbour at Copenhagen was further protected by a boom to control entry, as mentioned in 1294 (Nielsen 1872, 33: 56, 86) and in 1594 it was listed as a job of the customs officer at the *Tolhus* to raise and lower the boom every day and night (Nielsen 1872, 571: 481).

Proximity to local markets is something that can also be attributed to the majority of weighing houses, and the location of the weighing houses on Gammel Strand south of the markets at *Amagertorv* and *Gammeltorv* (modern names) meant Gammel Strand was in a perfect location for the trading in the city.

Construction of the harbour zone and creation of private and public areas

This section will investigate how the weighing houses existed within the surrounding harbour zone area. As discussed in the previous section, the location of weighing houses differed within each community or town. The area that became the harbour zone at present day Gammel Strand was created by a long and gradual period of construction. Between the years 1200 and 1400 the area between the streets *Læderstræde* to present-day Gammel Strand was created by land reclamation. Evidence for this is derived from bulwarks located on Naboløs street (in between Læderstræde and Gammel Strand) with dendrochronological dates of after 1260, 1324 and 1396, and at Gammel Strand after 1270 and *c.* 1332 (Jensen & Søndergård 2003; Bork-Petersen 2008). These bulwarks represented the construction of the new merchant-type harbour, which was possibly known as *Gammelbodehavn* (Old booth harbour) (Fabricius 1999, 153). It is likely that this early harbour comprised temporary booths, presumably for storage and selling goods, and some type of tax control building or room existed in the city. This area then appears to have become the location of private housing as the port moved southwards, and the land became free for use.

Evidence of the people living in the neighbourhood in the high medieval period may be found from residual finds of the later medieval and early post-medieval period from land reclamation and harbour base deposits. The finds suggest a real mixture of both high status and low-status goods amongst the assemblage with trading networks represented from central and northwestern Europe. Finds representing high status society include *Fadenrippenbecher* glass from Bohemia (an extremely rare glass in the period; Fig. 3.11), fragments of Pingsdorf type ceramic horns from central Germany (Fig. 3.12). These were found amongst high medieval remains such as Copenhagen Early red ware, imported proto stoneware, Siegburg stoneware, and grey ware from Germany, and dietary remains such as cow, chicken and pig animal bones.

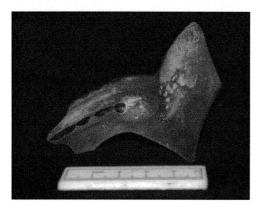

Fig. 3.11: Fadenrippenbecher Glass from Bohemia. Retrieved from mixed land reclamation deposits from the late 1600s (Museum of Copenhagen)

The Late Medieval harbour zone from 1400 to 1536 comprised at least two land reclamation episodes behind two different harbour-front bulwarks (Fig. 3.13), backfilled with rubbish representing Copenhagen society (Whatley *et al.* 2016, 126). There may have actually been another period of land reclamation, but this occurs at the end of high medieval/early Late Medieval period (Whatley *et al.* 2016, 86). It is in the Late Medieval period that we have the evidence from historical

Fig. 3.12: Pingsdorf type ceramic horn, 1200–1300. Retrieved from disturbed rubbish deposits at the harbour base in the late 1600s (Museum of Copenhagen)

Fig. 3.13: Oak posts from a Late Medieval bulwark located in the central area of the main excavation looking north-east (Museum of Copenhagen)

records and archaeological remains to suggest the area had a harbour zone set aside from the private housing area as no private housing was found on the Late Medieval harbourfront at Gammel Strand (Whatley *et al.* 2016, 125, 490).

The Late Medieval weighing house was possibly built at the time of the early- to mid-1400s' bulwarks. By this time, Møller writes that Gammel Strand was a bustling port with a row of houses along the northern side of the square which may have survived from the Late Medieval period until the great fire in 1795 (1988, 377). Fabricius (2006, 54) writes that the buildings on Gammel Strand during the medieval and early post-medieval periods were a mixture of large merchants' houses and noblemen's estates. Although these houses were located right next to the harbour they were not inhabited by people with harbour side professions such as rope makers, ships' clerks, skippers etc. who lived in the northwest of the city (Kjær 2008, 97–8). The inhabitants of Gammel Strand were people living in close proximity to the king on Slotsholmen, who had made Copenhagen the capital in the 1400s. This is shown through the finds material recovered from the former harbour base deposits (Fig. 3.14) and land reclamation behind the new harbour sides.

The harbour base deposits contained the same finds as seen in land reclamation, and as seen in the high medieval period revealed some high-status objects amongst everyday life artefacts. The finds show that the surrounding people retained their close networks and ties with Germany, the Netherlands and Belgium but added some new routes with, for example, figs being imported directly or indirectly from the Mediterranean (Whatley *et al.* 2016, 1451).

Fig. 3.14: Finely preserved Siegburg jugs found amongst Medieval rubbish discarded into the former harbour, c. 1300–1550 (Museum of Copenhagen)

The construction of the new weighing house in 1581 was one of many changes occurring in the area in the early post-medieval period. A new harbour wall was completed by 1583 (Fig. 3.15), which from the date of the storm posts of the bulwarks, may have started construction in 1567 (Whatley *et al.* 2016, 131–133). The wall itself represented great wealth as the foundation stones were brought in from all over Sjælland, with faced stone from the quarries at *Stevns Klint* and *munkesten* (Danish monk brick type) bricks fired near Copenhagen (Whatley *et al.* 2016, 134–138). In places, this new harbour wall was constructed on top of the Late Medieval bulwarks, but on a slightly different angle, thereby creating a larger harbourside area for storage and

Fig. 3.15: Photo of the 1583 harbour wall and the 1566/7 dendrochronologically dated bulwarks. Located at the eastern end of the main excavation looking north-east (Museum of Copenhagen)

Fig. 3.17: Base shard from a Chinese porcelain dish of Kraak type, c. 1580–1650. From land reclamation deposits 1640–1690 (Museum of Copenhagen)

Fig. 3.16: Glass stem of a 17th century Römer drinking vessel decorated with raspberry prunts. From an early post-medieval harbour base deposit (Haggrén 2016)

use. This arguably demonstrates public or governmental expenditure in the area.

The material culture during this period demonstrated a change in the trade networks and consumption by the surrounding population. Not only was there a larger quantity of finds, especially in glass and ceramics, but also a larger number of imported finds. Whereas, in the medieval periods, Germany was the major exporter to Copenhagen, by the late 1500s finds from the Netherlands were in equal quantity (Whatley *et al.* 2016, 156). This was seen especially in tableware items such as Majolica, lightly fired wares, faience plates, Chinese porcelain, cutlery and glass drinking vessels (Figs 3.16 and 3.17). Although stoneware was still imported in great numbers, the collection of *Römer glass* for wine and *Humpen* and *Pas glas* vessels (Haggrén 2016, 6–12) for beer celebrations were in high number. Households contained a larger number of prestige items such as pewter candle holders from chandeliers and stove tiles, and fashion changes were evident with shoes made from cork (used for soles) imported from Portugal (Vivi Andersen pers. comm.), a copper alloy headdress from a French-style hood (Whatley *et al.* 2016, 11). A higher status diet was also demonstrated from animal remains including young lambs (Bangsgaard *et al.* 2016, 28), fig seeds, and vessels for transport of wine and olive oil from Spain. Although there was an increase in high-status goods in the land reclamation deposits, there was also an increase in everyday goods. These must represent the waste from the servants and general workers living in the large town mansions, who were serving the elite owners. From the harbour base deposits, there was a similarity quantity of everyday and low-status goods. These goods not only represent the local society but may also represent the people using the harbour for work such as sailors and fishermen.

The pattern that emerges of the harbour of Gammel Strand is that over *c.* 350 years the harbour area probably separated into a public harbour-side zone and a private zone. The public harbour zone appears to have been in existence by the Late Medieval period (although knowledge of the High Medieval harbour area has yet to be found), and the weighing houses and storage areas for docks were constructed on the newly created land. The private buildings on Gammel Strand have not moved southwards from their current location since the mid-1400s, as demonstrated from excavations and seen on the first map of Copenhagen in the 1590s. The inhabitants were people more likely involved with governing the city and perhaps with trade than those who worked on the harbour-side.

Conclusion

Although the need for a weighing house in Copenhagen was first documented in 1281, such a building was not mentioned again in historical records until the period between the years 1450–1500, shortly after the city became the capital of Denmark. Weighing and taxing of goods must have occurred in other public buildings in the high medieval period, but these buildings or indeed a high medieval weighing house have yet to be identified. The presence of the king and his entourage in the city from the 1400s must have increased trade and wealth and led to the need for a new weighing house, which is represented by the Late Medieval weighing house in this article.

The Late Medieval weighing house lasted perhaps a hundred years and was located in what appears to be a newly created, and defined, public harbour zone. It worked alongside a toll-house to facilitate trade and tax goods in the harbour. The building itself was probably not a success. Due to the location of the building on newly created land, the floors and perhaps the property was possibly affected by damp as seen from the cellar and replacement of wooden floors.

By the 1580s the whole harbour was reconstructed. Stone harbour walls were constructed, with an increased area created for storage and a brand new, larger weighing house to cope with increased trade. Copenhagen was expanding and becoming a Scandinavia metropolis, and so the new weighing house became an ostentatious visual image of the increasingly wealthy capital city. With the king living on *Slotsholmen* since the 1400s, the surrounding houses became a wealthy neighbourhood full of town mansions, inhabited by the elite, taking advantage of the new high-status goods imported to the harbour of Copenhagen.

Bibliography

Ayers, B. (2016) *The German Ocean, Medieval Europe around the North Sea*, Sheffield/Bristol, Equinox.
Bangsgaard, P., Magnussen, B., Enghoff, I., Schonfeld, C., & Yeomans, L. (2016) Gammel Strand Z.M.K. 57/2011. Faunal Report KBM 3828. Unpublished report, Museum of Copenhagen

Evans, D. (1997) Hull archaeological work in the medieval port of Kingston-upon-Hull. In M. Gläser *Lübecker Kolloquium zur Stadtarchäologie im Hanseraum I: Stand, Aufgaben und Perspektiven*, 35–50. Lubeck, Schmit-Römhild.

Fabricius, H. (1999) Development of town and harbour in Medieval Copenhagen. In J. Bill & B. Clausen *Maritime Topography and the Medieval Town. Papers from the 5th International Conference on Waterfront Archaeology in Copenhagen*, 221–236. Studies in Archaeology & History Vol. 4. Copenhagen, The National Museum.

Fabricius, H. (2006) *Gader og mennesker i middelalderens & renæssancens København. Inden for middelaldervolden.* Copenhagen, Aschehoug.

de Graauw, J. (2011) De middeleeuwse bouwgeschiedenis van de Amsterdamse Sint-Anthonispoort. De Waag op de Nieuwmarkt nader onderzocht. *Bulletin Koninklijke Nederlandse Oudheidkundige Bond* 110, 3–4.

Haggrén, G. (2016) Gammel Strand glass finds, KBM 3828. Unpublished report, Museum of Copenhagen.

Jensen, J. & Søndergaard, M. (2003) Udfor Gammel Strand 52, Naboløs 5, samt Snaregade 4-8, KBM 2747. Unpublished report, Museum of Copenhagen.

Kjær, L. (2008) Københavns sociale topografi mellem 1400 of 1499. Speciale i faget historie, Københavns Universitet.

Kowalski, W. (2016) *The Great Immigration: Scots in Cracow and Little Poland, circa 1500-1660.* Leiden-Boston, Brill.

Milne, G. (1999) Marine topography & Medieval London. In J. Bill & B. Clausen *Maritime Topography and the Medieval Town. Papers from the 5th International Conference on Waterfront Archaeology in Copenhagen*, 145–152. Studies in Archaeology & History Vol. 4. Copenhagen, The National Museum.

Milne, G. (2006) *The Port of Medieval London.* Stroud, Tempus.

Møller, J. (1988) *København før og nu - og aldrig: Bind 3, Strøget og Gammel Strand.* Copenhagen, Palle Fogtdal.

Neale, F. (2000) *William Worcestre: The Topography of Medieval Bristol.* Bristol, Bristol Record Society.

Nielsen, O. (ed.) (1872) Kjøbenhavns Diplomatarium I. Copenhagen, Thiele. http://www.eremit.dk/ebog/kd/1/kd_1.html. (Accessed 06.10.2016).

Nielsen, O. (ed.) (1874) Kjøbenhavns Diplomatarium II. Copenhagen, Thiele. http://www.eremit.dk/ebog/kd/2/kd_2.html. (Accessed 06.10.2016)

Nielsen, O. (ed.) (1877a) Kjøbenhavns Diplomatarium III. Copenhagen, Thiele. http://www.eremit.dk/ebog/kd/3/kd_3.html. (Accessed 06.10.2016).

Nielsen, O. (ed.) (1877b) Kjøbenhavn Historie og Beskrivelse I. Kjøbenhavn i Middelalderen. Copenhagen, G. E. C. Gad. http://www.eremit.dk/ebog/khb/1/index.html. (Accessed 06.10.2016).

Nielsen, O. (ed.) (1879a) Kjøbenhavns Diplomatarium IV. Copenhagen, Thiele. http://www.eremit.dk/ebog/kd/4/kd_4.html. (Accessed 06.10.2016).

Nielsen, O. (ed.) (1881) Kjøbenhavn Historie og Beskrivelse III. Kjøbenhavn i Aarene 1536–1660 - første del. Copenhagen, G. E. C. Gad. http://www.eremit.dk/ebog/khb/3/index.html. (Accessed 06.10.2016).

Olesen, C. & Bork-Pedersen, K. (2012) Gammel Strand excavations 2010, KBM 3828. Unpublished report, Museum of Copenhagen.

Paner, H. (1999) Gdansk. Archaeological evidence for trade in Gdansk from the 12th to the 17th centuries. In M. Gläser *Lübecker Kolloquium zur Stadtarchäologie im Hanseraum II: Der Handel*, 387–402. Lubeck, Schmit-Römhild.

Rosenkjær, N. (1902) Fra Gammel Strand. Unpublished report in Museum of Copenhagen's archaeological archive, dated October 25th 1902.

Smidt, C. (1902) Notes from an excavation outside Gammel Strand 44, 46 and 48. NM 2. Afd. 295/01[?]. Unpublished report, in Nationalmuseet's archive, Copenhagen.

Söderlund, K. (1999) Trading city Stockholm- from the thirteenth to seventeenth centuries. In M. Gläser *Topography and Catchment Area. Lübecker Kolloquium zur Stadtarchäologie im Hanseraum II: Der Handel,* 505–512. Lubeck, Schmit-Römhild.
Wardas-Lason, M. & Garbacz-Klempka, A. (2016) Historical metallurgical activities and environment pollution at the substratum level of the main market square in Krakow. *Geochronometria* 43, 59–73.
Whatley, S., Haarby Hansen, C. & Morgan, R. (2016) Gammel Strand Metro Cityring project, KBM 3828. Unpublished report, Museum of Copenhagen.

Chapter 4

Medieval roof trusses in the Swedish landscape of Västergötland

Robin Gullbrandsson

This paper deals with the results of an inventory made in 2014–2015, with the aim to survey the extent of preservation of medieval roof constructions in church attics of the Diocese of Skara, part of the landscape Västergötland in western Sweden (Gullbrandsson 2015). More or less intact roof trusses from the 12th century up until the first half of the 13th century seem to be scarcely preserved outside Scandinavia, which increases the importance of mapping this quite unknown heritage in Sweden (Linscott 2007). The fact that we are dealing with wooden constructions in use for almost a thousand years is worth noting. Similar surveys have been made in five other dioceses during the same time and are about to be made in Linköping and Gothenburg, thus giving us a more complete view of the level of preservation (Eriksson and Borg 2014; Gullbrandsson 2014; 2017; Melin 2015; Taawo 2015; Eriksson and Torgén 2016).

Scandinavia has a large number of highly authentic churches from the period 1100–1350, a fact partly explained by the political and economic history in subsequent centuries. Reference has often been made to 'the importance of the Swedish poverty' and the absence of large-scale war damage in modern time. Among the medieval churches in Scandinavia are 22 stave churches and nine timber churches which constitute a well-known heritage (Gullbrandsson 2014, 78). It is less well known that beyond the *c.* 1300 – whole or partly intact – stone churches of the period there are a considerable number of preserved roof structures.

Earlier research

The first attempts to interpret medieval roof trusses were made in the early 20th century followed by the surveys made by the National Board of Antiquities in 'Churches of Sweden' which brought new knowledge, but was only able to study a fraction of the

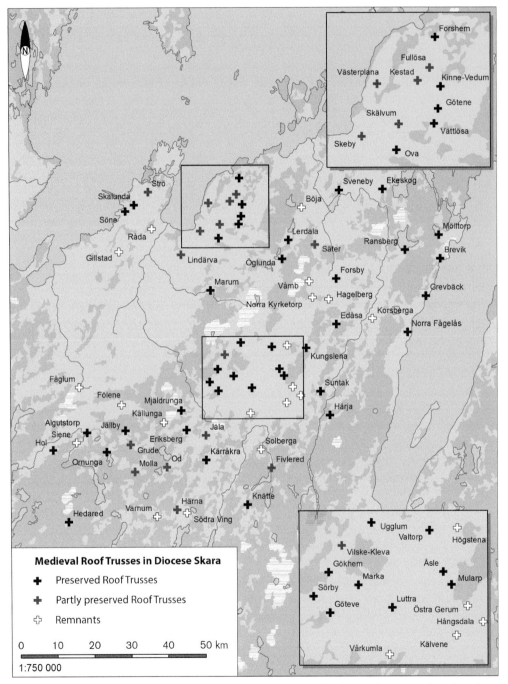

Fig. 4.1: Map of the Swedish landscape Västergötland, showing churches with preserved medieval roof trusses or traces of such. Black crosses indicate preserved ones, grey partly preserved and white traces (Ingvar Röjder, Jönköping County Museum)

total number of medieval churches. In an article from 1937 the art historian and head of the National Board of Antiquities, Sigurd Curman, pointed out the unique corpus of preserved medieval timber structures in the attics of Swedish churches as 'testimonies of a highly developed domestic carpentry awaiting its methodical investigation' (Curman 1937, 194). The art historian and architect Erik Lundberg took a vivid interest in timber architecture and presented in the 1940s quite daring conclusions concerning the origins and evolution of roof trusses (Lundberg 1940; 1949; 1971).

The emergence of dendrochronology in the 1970s and 1980s brought new interest to the medieval roof trusses as a means of scientifically dating of buildings. Analyses were performed on samples from several churches in Västergötland and other landscapes in southern Sweden (Bråthen 1995). The oldest yet dated standing roof construction in Sweden belongs to the church of Herrestad in Östergötland, erected around 1112 (Eriksson 2016, 43ff).

Besides the traditional perspectives of archaeology and art history, a new kind of approach is becoming established in the study of roof trusses and other historical timber structures. This is a craftsman perspective and was introduced in Peter Sjömar's thesis from 1988 (Sjömar 1988). The craftsman perspective has found its application in the investigations and practical experiments carried out by the craft school Hantverkslaboratoriet, linked to the Department of Conservation, University of Gothenburg, and the Södra Råda Project, the reconstruction of a burnt-down 14th-century timber church in Värmland. The constructions are viewed through the eyes of the carpenter, evaluating the processes of their creation, going from interpretation via re-enactment to re-interpretation (http://craftlab.gu.se/kunskapsbank/publikationer/sodra-rada-projektet, Accessed 05.09.2017; http://traditionsbararna.se/, accessed 05.09.2017).

With the creation of a database in 2007, the architect Kristina Linscott, University of Gothenburg, set out to map the known medieval roof structures in Swedish churches. This emphasized the need for methodical national surveys, in order to create a basis for scientific studies and to safeguard the future preservation of the delicate material. The database led to the supposition that the Swedish material may consist of some one hundred Romanesque roof structures and probably almost a hundred Gothic structures (Linscott 2007). Until the undertaking of the aforementioned surveys, our knowledge of the number of preserved objects was scarce and more or less random. As it presently stands, it seems that the medieval roof structures of churches in the landscapes of Götaland (mainly Västergötland, Östergötland and Småland) may comprise the largest preserved corpus of this kind from the 12th and 13th centuries in northern Europe.

The results of the survey

The Diocese of Skara has 164 churches with medieval origins, originally there were around 500 (Dahlberg 2002, 182). They are all situated in the old landscape of Västergötland. The purpose of the actual survey was to get a complete view of the

Fig. 4.2: Crossed strut-beam roof trusses over the nave in Sveneby church (Author)

extent of preserved material still standing as constructions, primarily in order to get a basis for the safeguarding of an easily tampered or destroyed material. The project was undertaken on the initiative of the diocese and financed with state funds. Of these 164 churches, 94 were visited. The others had, according to archival studies, been the object of large-scale enlargement, reconstruction or fire after the 16th century. For each visit, a maximum of four hours was envisaged, thus setting the level of the documentation. This was sufficient for the purpose of the survey (Gullbrandsson 2015, 9). Of course, there can still be unknown remnants of medieval construction, parts reused in later constructions, that can give much information.

The survey has identified whole or partly preserved medieval roof constructions and traces of such in the attics of almost 70 churches (Fig. 4.1). 28 roofs can be regarded as well-preserved roof trusses with tie beams, dating from the 12th century and the first half of the 13th century. 10 are only partly preserved and 18 were reused as part of later constructions (Gullbrandsson 2015, 370).

The majority of the examined churches are concentrated in the area around Kinnekulle and Falbygden as well as the neighbouring area southwest of the Cambro-Silurian landscape, the former oak forests of Edsveden. Large-scale modernization and demolitions during the 18th and 19th centuries have largely affected the level of preservation, thus leaving large areas of the diocese with hardly any traces of the medieval wooden constructions. It should be mentioned that reused or preserved

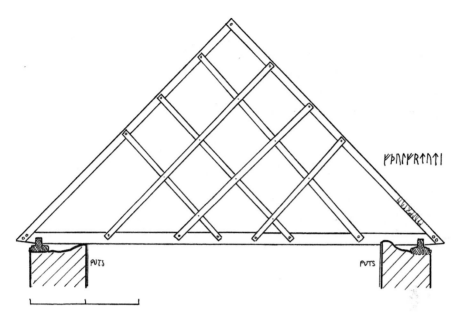

Fig. 4.3: Crossed strut-beam roof truss over the nave of Marum church, dated with dendrochronology to the 1140s. One of the rafters carved with runes: 'f th ulfr toti', probably the name of one of the carpenters erecting the roof (Author)

medieval parts can still appear in the attics or foundations, even of 19th-century churches.

Generally, the medieval roof structures have been categorized as Romanesque or Gothic, which actually has rather little to do with chronology, Romanesque types can be found even in the 18th century as well as Gothic ones. For simplicity, here we will nevertheless use these common terms. The Romanesque roof structure originally did not only have the practical function of supporting the roof, but was also an integral part of the church interior and thus an important element in the architectural and liturgical aesthetic. After the 13th century, the trusses were commonly hidden by flat wooden ceilings, later sometimes vaults. The angle of the roofs varies between 45 and 55 degrees and the material is usually pine and to a minor extent fir. Oak has mainly been used for wall plates and other exterior elements.

The most 'classic' of the Romanesque roof trusses consists of a tie beam, rafters and two to six interlacing strut beams, thus named 'crossed strut-beam roof truss' (Figs 4.2 and 4.3). The trusses rest on heavy wall plates, which are embedded in the top of the masonry, facing outwards. The different parts of the truss are joined by straight overleafing with wrought iron nails or wooden pegs. Usually, there are wooden pegs in the joints with the heavy tie beam, the most important load carrier, and nails in the others. Sometimes these pegs are shaped like nails, indicating the exclusiveness of the iron. The crossed strut-beam trusses are well represented in the

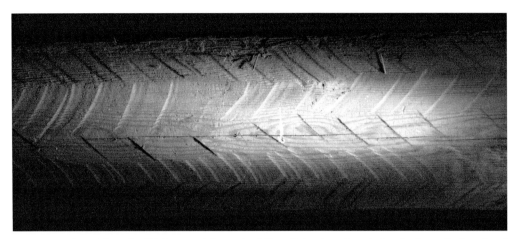

Fig. 4.4: Cutting with sprättäljning on tie beam in oblique lightning, Kestad church, the wall plate dated with dendrochronology to 1131 (Author)

landscapes around lake Vättern: Västergötland, Östergötland and Småland in the 12th and even the 13th century.

What all of these Romanesque trusses have in common is the technique of cutting. All elements are carefully cut to square angles with an axe and a technique cutting along the fibres, known as *sprättäljning*, leaving unmistakable traces, a type of fishbone pattern leaping in even bands along the whole piece (Fig. 4.4). Sometimes this pattern has vanished since the surface was afterwards planed with a draw-knife or hewn with a broader axe in different angle according to the practice in for example Denmark and Germany, thus getting an even smoother surface. Hewing by *sprättäljning* has come to be regarded as a characteristic of medieval timbering in Scandinavia by several researchers (Sjömar 1992; 1995; Storsletten 2002, 8, 316). Sometime during the 14th century, however, it vanished and was replaced with a cruder technique, hard to distinguish from works of early modern times, thus making the pure stylistic dating of Gothic structures problematic. The Norwegian Storsletten has also argued that *sprättäljning* could have been a prehistoric Nordic technique applied to the new churches, considering the fact that the techniques of handling the timber did not change from the earliest preserved examples up until around mid-14th century (Storsletten 2002, 8).

Did local timber craftsmen merge with the imported masons in the early building of Romanesque stone churches during the 12th century? Lundberg and others claimed that the use of roof trusses was a medieval introduction in Scandinavia, a framework enabling the roof structure to span a broad space without supports other than the outer walls (Lundberg 1971, 143). A preserved parallel to the Swedish crossed strut-beam truss is to be found in Chabris in France, which also exemplifies that this type was not purely a Scandinavian invention (Hoffsummer 2011, 323–325). It is plausible that the main elements of the early Romanesque roof trusses were

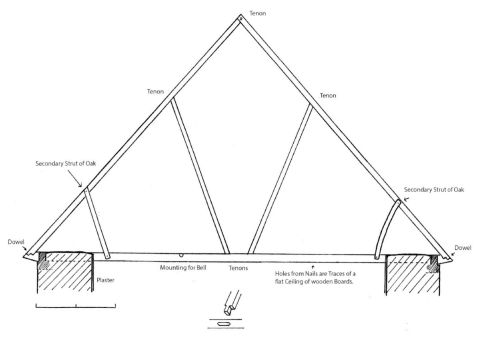

Fig. 4.5: Roof truss with two canted struts with tenons in the nave of Götene church. Wall plates in the choir dated with dendrochronology to the 1120s (Author)

introduced from abroad but merged with Nordic carpenter traditions. Sjömar and Storsletten, though, have stressed the emergence of regional carpenter traditions (Sjömar 1995, 226; Storsletten 2002).

Some of the medieval churches in the diocese have been dated with dendrochronology and they span from the 1110s (chancel of Kungslena) up until around 1250 (Ornunga nave). A group of roof trusses with two canted struts (often meeting the rafters and tie beam with tenons) seems to belong to the oldest period, though these are only partly preserved in a few churches mainly around Kinnekulle (for example Götene from the 1120s, Fig. 4.5). The most common type of roof trusses has crossed struts, the most advanced of them boasts six (for example Forsby nave 1135, Gökhem nave c. 1140 (Fig. 4.6), Marum nave 1140s and Mjäldrunga nave after 1201) and the simplest only two struts (for example above the timbered nave of Jällby). Some of these roof trusses have decorative features like profiled ridge purlins (Fig. 4.7) or steering plates, which to a larger extent can be found in Småland and Östergötland. In several churches, there are traces of mountings for liturgical bells (Fig. 4.8). These facts clearly show that the earliest stone churches did not have ceilings. It was probably common that the exterior wall plates (Fig. 4.9) were decorated and there are traces of decorated ridges and wind discs. Timber markings are very rare in this material. In the church of Marum though, one of the carpenters have obviously signed his work. Four medieval tower roofs have been preserved in Härja, Kinne-Vedum, Sörby

Fig. 4.6: Detail of crossed strut-beams with decorate joints in the nave of Gökhem church, dated with dendrochronology to c. 1140 (Author)

and Öglunda. Another project has identified seven medieval belfries in the diocese (Bygdén *et al.* 2014).

Very few constructions are preserved from the end of the 13th century until the beginning of the 16th century. There probably never existed any great number because of the economic and political decline for Västergötland after the plague and agrarian crisis in the mid-14th century. Roof trusses from these centuries exist today in 13 churches, with a clear concentration along the coastline of Lake Vättern, an area that was dominated by the Cistercian monastery of Alvastra on the Östergötland side of the lake. Here we find four gothic churches with pointed roofs. These constructions

Fig. 4.7: Decorate ridge purlin in the nave of Ljungsarp church (Author)

Fig. 4.8: The tie beams of the choir in Kinne-Vedum church have traces for mountings of liturgical bells. Wall plate in the nave dated to 1186–1188 (Author)

Fig. 4.9: Romanesque relief on wall plate of the choir in Skalunda church. The roof structure of the nave is dated to 1145-1148 (Author)

are large in comparison with the ones encountered in the earlier Medieval churches of the diocese.

We still lack a complete survey of Götaland, and the fact that a large number of churches have been torn down or rebuilt limits the conclusions that can be drawn. Today we can only see a fraction of how widespread different types of roof trusses were in time and space. Nonetheless, we can now say that we have quite a good knowledge of the original constructions in one sixth of all the existing and vanished medieval churches of the diocese of Skara. The Romanesque crossed strut-beam trusses can be found in large parts of medieval Götaland, in effect the landscapes around lake Vättern.

The ongoing surveys in Sweden will certainly enlarge the empirical material considerably, giving us a more complete picture of what has been preserved in the church attics. This will enable the modification of the present questions and form the basis for new ones. Further studies in specific roof structures, in combination with dendrochronological analysis, will yield important data for creating a typology and a chronology for the Swedish material. In the end, better knowledge may contribute to the preservation of a unique but long-neglected heritage.

Bibliography

Bråthen, A. (1995) *Dated Wood from Gotland and the Diocese of Skara*. Højbjerg, Hikiun.

Bygdén, B., Eriksson, D., Hallgren, M. & Krantz, E. O. (2014) *Klockstaplar i Skara stift. Rapport från en pilotstudie 2012-2014. Timmermännens perspektiv*. Skara, Västergötlands museum.

Curman, S. (1937) Två romanska träkonstruktioner. In S Curman (ed.) *Från stenålder till rokoko. Studier tillägnade Otto Rydbeck den 25 augusti 1937*, 183–95. Lund, Geerups.

Dahlberg, M. (ed.) (2002) *Västergötland - landskapets kyrkor. Sockenkyrkorna - kulturarv och bebyggelsehistoria.* Stockholm, Riksantikvarieämbetet.

Eriksson, D. & Borg, A. (2014) *Medeltida kyrkotaklag. Örebro län, Strängnäs stift. Inventering etapp 1, 2013-2014. Rapport 2014:05.* Örebro, Örebro läns museum.

Eriksson, D. & Torgén, C. (2016) *Medeltida kyrkotaklag. Örebro län, Strängnäs stift. Etapp 2, 2015-2016. Rapport 2016:04.* Örebro, Örebro läns museum.

Eriksson, J. (2006) *Dendrokronologiska undersökningar av medeltida kyrkor inom Linköpings stift.* Länsstyrelsen i Östergötlands län, Linköping.

Gullbrandsson, R. (2014) Medieval Roof Trusses in Churches of Northern Småland. *Lund Archaeological Review* 19, 77–94.

Gullbrandsson, R. (2015) *Medeltida taklag i Skara stifts kyrkor.* Skara, Skara stiftshistoriska sällskap.

Gullbrandsson, R. (2017) *Medeltida taklag i Göteborgs stifts kyrkor - en förstudie.* Västarvet, Vänersborg.

Hoffsummer, P. (ed.) (2011) *Les charpentes du XIe au XIXe siècle. Grand Ouest de la France.* Turnhout, Brepols.

Linscott, K. (2007) *Medeltida tak. Bevarade takkonstruktioner i svenska medeltidskyrkor. Rapport om kunskapsläget 2006.* Göteborg, Göteborgs universitet.

Lundberg, E. (1940) *Byggnadskonsten i Sverige. Under medeltiden: 1000-1400.* Stockholm, Nordisk rotogravyr.

Lundberg, E. (1949) *Arkitekturens formspråk. Studier över arkitekturens konstnärliga värden i deras historiska utveckling. 3. Västerlandets medeltid: 600-1200.* Stockholm, Nordisk rotogravyr.

Lundberg, E. (1971) *Trä gav form. Studier över byggnadskonst vars former framgått ur trämaterial och träkonstruktion.* Stockholm, Norstedts.

Melin, K.-M. (2015) *Historisk timmermanskonst i Lunds stift. Nomenklatur och bildkompendium.* https://timmermanskonst.wordpress.com/category/lunds-stift/ (Accessed 09.05.2017).

Sjömar, P. (1988) *Byggnadsteknik och timmermanskonst. En studie med exempel från några medeltida knuttimrade kyrkor och allmogehus.* Göteborg, Chalmers.

Sjömar, P. (1992) Romanska takkonstruktioner – ett värdefullt och outforskat källmaterial. In M. Ullén (ed.), *Från romanik till nygotik. Studier i kyrklig konst och arkitektur tillägnade Evald Gustafsson,* 56–66. Stockholm, Riksantikvarieämbetet.

Sjömar, P. (1995) Romanskt och gotiskt – takkonstruktioner i svenska medeltidskyrkor. *Hikuin* 22, 207–30. Kirkearkæologi i Norden.

Storsletten, O. (2002) *Takene taler. Norske takstoler 1100-1350 klassifisering og oprinnelse.* Oslo, Arkitekthøgskolen i Oslo.

Taawo, K. (2015) *Medeltida taklag i Södermanland. Inventering och dokumentation 2014. Södermanlands museums rapport 2015:7.* Nyköping, Sörmlands museum.

Chapter 5

The medieval hospitals of England: Structuring charity and faith through hierarchies of space

Martin Huggon

The medieval hospitals of England

The medieval hospitals of England were a distinct institution that spanned a period of over 450 years, proving to be a varied but popular form of social welfare and religious activity that provided shelter and food to the vulnerable, poor, and outsiders of medieval society. The first two documented hospitals in England were established by Lanfranc, Archbishop of Canterbury, in the 1080s, and it was only with the passing of the Chantry's Act of 1547 by Edward VI, abolishing the role of intercessionary prayers that were a feature of many medieval hospitals, that the increasing differences observable between medical hospitals and almshouses split them apart as institutions. Between the Conquest of 1066 and the ascension to the English throne by Edward VI, at least 1,200 hospitals and almshouses (treated here together under the term hospital) were active. Some lasted no more than a few years, whilst others, such as the Hospital of St John the Baptist, Canterbury, founded in the 1080s and which survived the 1547 Act, provided charitable care for centuries. As such, it is legitimate to assume that the concept of the 'hospital' would have been as familiar to contemporary society as the idea of the 'monastery' (Watson 2006, 76). In England there is no unequivocal evidence of the hospital before the 1080s, leading to the argument that the Continental form of the medieval hospital was introduced by the Normans to formalise the Anglo-Saxon ideas on charity and support of the poor, sick, and infirm already active (Watson 2006). Although *hospitalis* grew to be the dominant term for these sites after its first use in 1112 it was a descriptive term, not a constitutional one as it was on the Continent, and the use of ecclesiastical or monastic terminology in hospital foundation texts and documents was rare (Watson 2006, 79). This indicates that English hospitals were not conceived of as monastic houses or entirely followed the wider European hospital traditions (see for example

Leistikow 1967 for this more traditional approach), but potentially had their own distinctive form that added elements of Anglo-Saxon religious and social ideology.

Hospitals derive their name from the Latin *hospitalis*, a concern for *hospites* (guests), and under this broad definition an institution formed across medieval Europe that offered assistance to the needy through the basic Christian doctrine of charity, often in return for intercessionary prayers for founders, benefactors, and residents (Clay 1909; Dainton 1976, 532; Rawcliffe 1984, 2; Carlin 1989, 21; Gilchrist 1995, 8; Buklijaš 2008). This charity was grounded specifically in the Seven Comfortable Acts of Jesus Christ, namely to feed the poor, clothe the poor, bring drink, house wayfarers, visit prisoners, nurse the sick, and bury the dead, and each site was heavily dependent on remaining a viable element of the spiritual economy for continuing benefaction and gifts, particularly from the secular middle class (Clay 1909; Rowe 1958, 257; Gilchrist 1995; Orme & Webster 1995; Sweetinburgh 2004; Watson 2006, 76; Roberts 2007; Buklijaš 2008). Their scope was often wide-ranging, with some element of a religious rule and following the monastic vows and daily routine. Communities could comprise a mix of religious and secular residents, men and women, the wealthy and the poor, and as such have proven an important source for the wider study of medieval piety, power dynamics, charity, medicine, health and healing, death and burial, social needs, and urban politics (for example Rawcliffe 1995; 2006; Gilchrist & Sloane 2005; McIntosh 2012). Although there seems to have been a strict sexual, and in all likelihood social, segregation of space and activity (Dainton 1976, 533; Carlin 1989, 24; Gilchrist 1995, 11, 14, 16; Rawcliffe 1995, 207), architectural studies of standing remains dominated the discourse (Godfrey 1955; Prescott 1992; Orme & Webster 1995).

The archaeological contribution to such discussions includes how types of resident affected the site layout, how sites usually grow organically, the poor quality of construction, organisation, and status compared to other religious institutions, or the relationship between the two central pillars of the hospital: the infirmary hall, as the residence of those receiving the charity; and the chapel, as the centre of faith on the site (Gilchrist 1995; Thomas *et al.* 1997; Price & Ponsford 1998; Roberts 2007; Atkins & Popescu 2010; Roffey 2012). Where more generalised comments about layout have been made, such as by Orme and Webster (1995, 86–90), who discuss the use of cloisters and courtyards to organise space, the focus is either upon the division of space functionally or as a dichotomy between religious and secular space but without referencing how these two areas interacted and are located in relation to each other. Ultimately this has led to the conclusion that as a national institution 'the hospital possessed an undefined, unruly, shifting and quasi-monastic form ... spectral, a concept within social discourse', rather than a clearly defined institution (Watson 2006, 76–77). By ignoring the important role other buildings in the hospital precinct played in organising activity and daily life, such as kitchens, staff quarters, gardens, and workshops, there is a lack of coherent base-line from which comparisons and differences can be judged, hindering wider debate. The following chapter proposes a preliminary methodological framework for analysing how the medieval hospital may have been structured intentionally, discussed through the case study of three English hospital sites: two urban sites, St Mary Spital, London, and St Bartholomew's, Bristol; and one rural site, St Mary's, Ospringe, Kent.

Hospital architecture as a complex for charity and faith

When examining the medieval hospital most of the focus has fallen on the infirmary hall and the chapel, firstly due to survival or excavation bias, and secondly because these two buildings represent the core pillars of the hospital: charity and faith. The infirmary hall or inmates' dormitory was the location of care at a hospital site, usually comprising a rectangular hall, sometimes referred to as a nave, complete with beds for the inmates, with separation of the sexes via partitions, separate storeys, or completely separate buildings (Carlin 1989, 28; Prescott 1992, 5). The chapel is traditionally seen as located to the east of the infirmary hall, directly communicating or open to the nave, allowing the inmates to witness the daily celebration of the mass from their beds (Carlin 1989, 28; Gilchrist 1995, 17; Rawcliffe 1995, 210). However, it is clear this was not always the case, particularly with the addition of a number of extensively excavated hospitals over the past 30 years added to those already known from architectural studies. For example, at St Giles Hospital, Brompton Bridge (Cardwell 1995), or St Mary Magdalen Hospital, Winchester (Roffey 2012), the infirmary hall is separate and parallel to the chapel or located in another area of the site. Documentary records indicate that a mobile altar to St Nicholas was used in the infirmary hall of St Mary Spital (Thomas *et al.* 1997, 48), which may have been a common way to provide spiritual care to the inmates. Certainly, the layout of other hospitals, such as the hospitals of St Giles, Norwich, St John the Baptist, Canterbury, and St Mary the Virgin, Strood, the former with a parish nave between the infirmary hall and the chapel, and the latter two having a north–south infirmary hall with the chapel opening out to the east from the middle of the hall, would have precluded vision or active engagement with ceremonies in the chapel (Orme and Webster 1995, 89–90; Rawcliffe 1999).

Rather than arguing for the sole importance of vision, Peregrine Horden asserts that hospitals were acting upon all the senses, both through liturgical music and chant as a form of therapeutic treatment (Horden 2001), but more generally through non-natural theory, a widespread extension of Galenic medical thought from Johannitius (Hunayn ibn Ishaq, died *c.* 877) where negative emotions, such as anger, lust, fear, and anxiety, could cause illness and other maladies (Horden 2007). Such 'accidents of the soul' impacted the humours and were influenced by the elements, and the medical remedy for them focussed on corrective diet, rest, and the creation of a joyous mind through prayer, confession, contemplation of God and his Works, mass, exposure to devotional imagery, and being in the presence of the raising of the Host. Horden (2007) argued that the environment of the hospital would have been an important element in the treatment of illness and malady for the poor, such as through access to, or to hear from, the chapel or by visits to the gardens, which were not just producers of foodstuffs and medicinal plants, but using scent, sight, and sound became a location of calm, spiritual reflection and contemplation on the redemptive sufferings of Christ. These practices were known to English hospitals, evident in their inclusion in the *Brevarium Bartholomei*, written by John Mirfield in the late 14th century, a canon of St Bartholomew's Hospital, London (Horden 2007, 144).

Medieval medicine more generally was focussed on prognosis, diet, the humoral balance, spiritual purity, and preparedness for the death of the patient (Rawcliffe 1995; 1999). This seems to be mirrored by the current scholarly view of hospitals as being *foci* of food, shelter, cleanliness, and warmth for the medieval poor and suffering, tied to a clear concern for the soul of the residents through the provision of confession, prayer, mass, sermons, preaching, provision for burial, and spiritual contemplation in the rules and admittance ordinances (Rowe 1958, 255; Carlin 1989, 31; Rubin 1989, 51; Gilchrist 1995, 32; Orme & Webster 1995; Rawcliffe 2006; Egan 2007, 76; Davis 2010). Physical medicine was rarely, if ever, the primary focus, as can be seen by the virtual absence of items of surgical or medical practice in English hospitals (Egan 2007). Rather, the medieval hospital provided a location where the poor could experience a level of medical care, diet, and religious lifestyle; in essence, the healthy regimen encouraged by physicians (as discussed by Sotres 1998), unobtainable for them outside the precinct walls (Agrimi & Crisciani 1998, 192). There is also an implication that this approach was beneficial to the poor who were not unwell, a group that made up the majority of residents at these sites particularly with the focus on the 'deserving poor' from the 14th century onwards (McIntosh 2012; Rawcliffe 1984). This implies that impious poverty was seen as a possible cause of sickness or sin that the spiritually nourishing lifestyle of the hospitals and almshouses could prevent.

This would mean that structuring the layout of the hospital to provide space for contemplation and create the environment of piety and order would be highly important, and the principle that buildings can impact in this way upon people's actions and perceptions of society has long been a topic of study (for example Bourdieu 1970). Buildings function as a system for convenient and self-repeating mythico-religious ideology that self-supports both the internal unit but also wider society more generally. Care must be taken to not overstep the interpretative boundary, and often the symbolic is over-emphasised in relation to the functional, when actually they are not mutually exclusive but rather, when combined, reflections of use; thus, something functional can still be symbolic. However, this approach indicates the potential buildings have for influencing their immediate residents and wider society. Space constricts and informs movement and activity via imbued meanings, actions and stories that are communicated through a series of signs and surfaces masking the overt imposition of power behind collective will and thought (Parker Pearson *et al.* 1994). By interacting with this negotiated environment, permanence of place is formed and tied to material markers. This permanence and form become bound despite, or more accurately *because,* that imbued meaning can be changed or manipulated (Parker Pearson & Richards 1994, 3–4). In essence, the imbuing of meaning is the *intent* of the site or layout, whilst the physical manifestation, interaction with or replication of these *intents* could be termed the *results*. *Intent* can be communicated through all the senses, and as such there is a heightened vitality and dynamic to the material nature of buildings, rather than just acting as inert and passive containers for action (Melhuish 2005, 10). Thus the 'experience' of this active architecture is culturally relevant (Parker Pearson *et al.* 1994, 4), but also culturally dependent on how the senses are structured to respond and provide information to the individual about their place in society and their personal knowledge of their culture (Melhuish 2005, 11). This splits the interpretation of the environment into the *intent* of a site's layout and the *result* of action, which can lead to very different experiences. The archaeological and historical record represent elements of both *intent* and *result*, and without appreciating the existence of both interpretation will be incomplete.

When considering medieval buildings, especially religious sites such as the hospital, it is important to recognise that the idea of similarity was not just focused on design and construction, but also symbolic significance and selected recreation of specific, important religious or ideological elements (Krautheimer 1942). Approximate similarity was satisfactory as long as the symbolic implications were also evident, symbolism accompanying form, and the process of creating 'the relation between pattern and symbolical meaning could be better described as being determined by a network of half-distinct connotations' that could have a multitude of meanings (Krautheimer 1942, 9). Diagnostic elements of a medieval building, such as the Holy Sepulchre at Jerusalem, could be distilled down to a few traits, such as shape, dedication, specific measurements, or some combination of architectural elements, and be built again in copies such as St Michael, Fulda, the Holy Sepulchre, Paderborn, or the Holy Sepulchre, Cambridge, where to a modern eye there is little similarity between them (Krautheimer 1942, 3–5, 15–16). As such, elements of the *intent* of the site will be evident, but they will be obscured by the *result* of the varied choices and histories of each site. It is already clear that direct similarity is not present at English hospitals, but it does not need to be when looking for a shared underlying framework, as long as there are some repeated elements of form that combine with the immaterial spiritual and charitable meanings already evident. This form will likely be influenced by contemporary medical theory, where diet and daily lifestyle in a positive religious environment were pivotal, as well as some reference to the template of monastic layouts as the most prevalent form to structure or order this hybrid secular-religious life.

It seems quite clear that, in theory, the layout and interaction of the different buildings in a hospital complex should be of key importance to the lives of the residents, and that there should be a general order to this layout. Indeed, this sentiment has been expressed by both historians, architects, and archaeologists, but without a general framework that explains how these sites all fall under the term 'hospital' physically (for example Clay 1909; Godfrey 1955; Carlin 1989; Gilchrist 1992; 1995; Prescott 1992; Orme and Webster 1995; Roberts 2007). By considering how the medieval hospitals acted as a complex for charity and faith and located the provision of alms, care, faith, and medical relief, it should be possible to observe a shared framework that reflects the *intent* and the *result* of their shared, although not necessarily identical, architectural layout. Whilst it will be argued here that there was an underlying grammar structuring how these sites were laid out, it is also obvious that significant levels of variation should be expected in the nature of the buildings, even without taking into account the differences in wealth between institutions, the alternate objectives in care, idiosyncratic individual site histories, reuse of old buildings, changing functions, luck, and the vagaries of survival. However, as discussed below in the examination of St Mary Spital, St Bartholomew's, and St Mary, Ospringe, a potential framework is apparent and may highlight how the medieval hospitals of England fit within an understanding of wider religious institutions.

The archaeology of English medieval hospitals: three case studies

St Mary Spital, London

The Hospital of St Mary Spital, London, was initially founded as a small roadside hostel outside Bishopsgate in 1197, only 15 m long on an east–west alignment (Thomas *et al.* 1997, 24–25). Refounded in 1235 on a much larger scale, St Mary Spital became the second largest hospital in England, eventually caring for 180 inmates, in particular travellers, migrant workers, mothers in childbirth, orphans, the sick, and the poor. The new hospital and priory initially comprised a T-shaped building, with a north and south ward, likely dividing the sexes, and a chancel running off to the east (Thomas *et al.* 1997, 28, 33). The combined wards were 51 × 16.4 m, with the chancel likely more than 30 m in length with the Lady Chapel included. Wear patterns on the floor of the wards indicate that the beds were located in the outer aisles, with space for around 60 inmates. A latrine attached to the east wall of the northern ward, complete with two chalk-lined cess-pits was likely mirrored in the southern ward, although later modification and truncation removed these elements (Thomas *et al.* 1997, 35–36). To the north of the northern ward, across an open space and some cultivated land that was later referred to as the Sisters' Garden, was Building 3, comprising a series of postholes and a mortar floor, interpreted as being the dormitory of the lay sisters on site, which was subsequently replaced with a larger building after it burnt down (Thomas *et al.* 1997, 36–39, 52–53). No canons' dormitory was located for this period, although it may have been truncated by the later cloister that was constructed just north of the chancel.

   In the 40 years either side of 1300 the site continued to develop (Fig. 5.1), with the inmates moved into a new building, Building 5, attached to the west wall of the north ward, which now became the transepts of the chapel (Thomas *et al.* 1997, 46–47). A doorway that would have connected the new infirmary hall with the transept was blocked up, meaning there was no direct connection between the two buildings, although there may have been windows between them. Building 5 was 22.3 × 11 m,

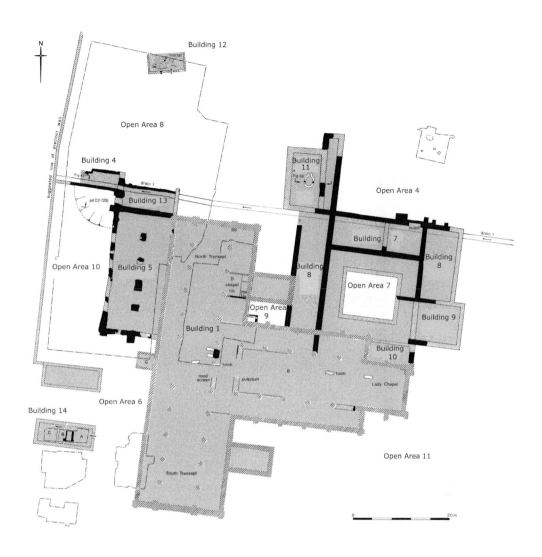

Fig. 5.1: Plan of the main archaeological features of St Mary Spital, c. 1280–1320. Note the location of Building 5, the Infirmary, in relation to Building 1, the chapel, and the cloister to the north (Adapted from Thomas et al. 1997, fig. 32. Reproduced with permission of the Museum of London Archaeology)

with thick walls and several buttresses on the northwest and southwest corners, implying that this was a two-storey building, possibly with the sexes on different floors, and would have maintained the capacity of inmates (Thomas *et al.* 1997, 48). A two-storey latrine, Building 13, was located against the north wall of the infirmary hall, and attached to the northwest corner of the latrine was Building 4, another latrine likely for the sisters (Thomas *et al.* 1997, 46, 50, 53). Excavations in the 1930s indicate it was in this period that the canons' cloister was built against the northern wall of the chapel, in a typical layout for an Augustinian house with the prior's lodging and guest house in the west range, a two-room refectory in the north range, with evidence for a possible pulpit, and a dormitory with a cellar underneath in the east range, with the chapter house to the south, connecting to the chapel and sacristy (Thomas *et al.* 1997, 48–51). The kitchen building, Building 11, was attached to the northern wall of the western range and appears to have been the main kitchen for the whole site, with passageways connecting to the infirmary hall to the west and the refectory to the east, and was supplied with water through the main drain of the site, running from east to west through most of the domestic buildings and the latrines. A large gatehouse was also built to the west of the southern transept and appears to have been the main entrance to the courtyard in front of the chapel.

The developments of the site over the next 220 years until the Reformation did not drastically alter the nature of how the site functioned (Fig. 5.2). Between 1320 and 1350 an extension to the infirmary hall was made to the entire western wall, virtually doubling the capacity of the site, as well as a large stables and workshop range that ran north from the northwest corner of this new extension (Thomas *et al.* 1997, 65–67). In the half century up to 1400 multiple changes, repairs, and modifications were made, some relating to structural failings, especially in the south transept (Thomas *et al.* 1997, 69, 74). The most significant changes for this discussion were the movement of the Sisters' quarters to a location against the northern walls of the north transept and infirmary hall, the slight shifting of the latrines to the west, the construction of workshops and an accommodation block for lay brethren and male servants, Building 21, to the northwest of the kitchen, and the addition to the kitchen area, likely serving as a pantry, bakery, and buttery range (Thomas *et al.* 1997, 70–74). An arcade appears to have been added to separate the Sisters' garden in the west, which also had a well and some gravel yard surfaces, from the kitchen garden in the east (Thomas *et al.* 1997, 75–76). The only observed addition in the final 140 years of the site's history was the addition of a tenement to the northern wall of the Sisters' Quarters, likely for corrodians, the continued modification of the chapel to mitigate structural failings and to enlarge the chancel and private chapels, and the construction of a passageway linking the kitchen directly to the Sisters' Refectory and infirmary hall, possibly caused by scandal in the 15th century (Thomas *et al.* 1997, 81, 84, 87).

What can be observed in these changes is the solidification of two spaces, one to the northwest of the chapel focussed on the infirmary hall, the Sisters' Quarters, and the stables, and the other that was located to the north and east of the chapel, with the cloister at its heart and touching on the lay brethren accommodation, the canons' infirmary and the prior's garden to the east. It is observable that these elements were planned from an early stage, and although some developments were dependent upon idiosyncrasies of the site, the split between the two areas, one male and religious, the other female and secular, seems clear from within 50 years of the refoundation of the hospital. It is unclear why the canons' cloister was placed to the north of the chapel rather than the south, especially given the large space available for the cemetery to the south and southeast (Connell *et al.* 2012). On its own, this creation of two such

N

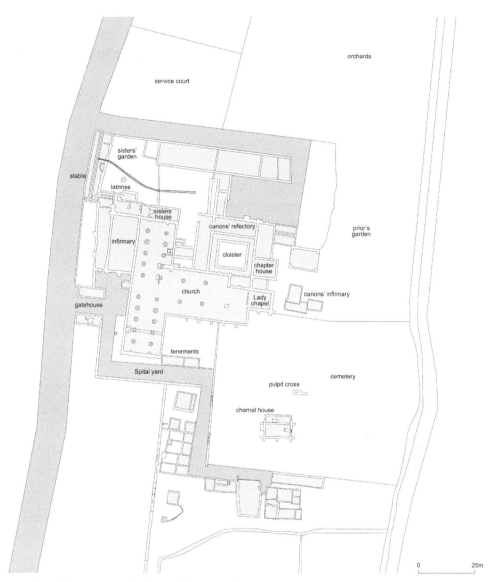

Fig. 5.2: Plan of the main archaeological features of St Mary Spital, c. 1400–1538. The eastern half of the site remained associated with the canons, whilst the western half continued to structure the lives of the inmates and female servants (Connell et al. 2012, 199, fig. 219. Reproduced with permission of the Museum of London Archaeology)

spaces can be explained by functional and practical reasons, such as there being more space to the north for buildings, the religious men would by necessity of their vows require clear separation from women working on site, the location of the kitchen between the two ranges would allow it to serve both sets of the community, and the movement of the inmates out of the transepts of the chapel allowed more space for private chapels and devotion that would serve as a useful source of income for an institution notable for its issues with money. Yet, the lack of major change in over 200 years despite scandal and major refurbishment may indicate that there was some intent behind the choice of location for these buildings.

St Bartholomew's Hospital, Bristol

Founded between the years 1232 and 1234 on the bank of the River Frome, St Bartholomew's Hospital suffered from the start with issues about finances and structural instability (Price & Ponsford 1998, 53, 78–79). The hospital was for a mixed community of perhaps 30 poor, although some illness and infirmity were inherent in the population admitted, and was run by a master, two chaplains, and an uncertain number of servants, likely of both sexes, living by the 14th century at the latest to an unclear but likely modified Augustinian Rule. In the first half-century of the hospital, the focus of the site was on stabilising and organising the pre-existing Norman hall, which had an undercroft that was later filled-in destroying the earlier evidence, and on the open ground just to the northwest, where Building 7 was located, a short-lived refectory or kitchen (Price & Ponsford 1998, 59, 62, 79–81). Later documentary sources from the 1340s noted an old women's dormitory to the north of the excavation area that was either constructed at this point or a little later, beyond which was the hospital cemetery and an area of cultivated land. In the decades around 1300 two new blocks were constructed, Building 8 and Building 2 (Fig. 5.3), the former only barely touched by the excavation but from the thickness of the walls a two-storey structure, likely the staff and guest quarters of the hospital, and the latter, on the evidence of animal bones and organic floor residues, the new refectory and kitchen range, with a possible staircase in the western room that may have led to dormitories above (Price & Ponsford 1998, 69-71, 74, 82–83). The fact that a drain supplied fresh water to Building 8 supports the idea this was an accommodation block, as does the path and garden features built over the demolished Building 7 between it and the gate to the east, whilst north of the path was a courtyard surface in front of Building 2. North of Building 2 was Building 3, possibly a brewhouse or bakehouse based on the evidence of the charcoal-rich floor deposits (Price & Ponsford 1998, 75, 84).

Other than the replacement of Building 3 with Building 4, a possible granary, and the construction of Building 5 to the east (Price & Ponsford 1998, 85–86), the only significant change to the site was carried out between 1340 and 1400 (Fig. 5.4). The original hall, likely serving as the chapel despite the odd alignment, had its undercroft filled in, a small chancel added onto the northeast wall, an extension was added against the northwest wall, and burials began inside the chapel (Price & Ponsford 1998, 90, 94–96). Also added were a staircase and columns that likely supported a gallery or half-floor over the western half of the chapel, whilst below it, a partition also seems to have blocked off the western half of the ground floor, with a kitchen hearth and some

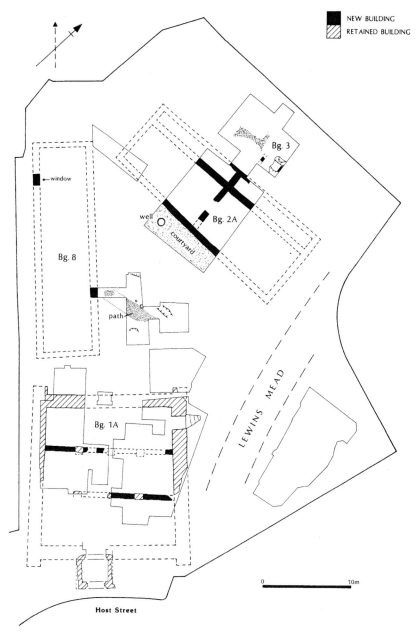

Fig. 5.3: Plan of the main archaeological features of St Bartholomew, Bristol, c. 1280–1320. The four sides of an irregular courtyard were formed by Building 1A (the chapel), Building 8 (the presumed guest quarters and staff dormitory), Building 2A (the kitchen and refectory), and Lewins Mead. To the north of Building 2A was a series of service buildings, as well as the Women's Dormitory (Price & Ponsford 1998, 64, fig. 23. Reproduced with permission of the Council for British Archaeology © Roger Price, Michael Ponsford, and the Council for British Archaeology)

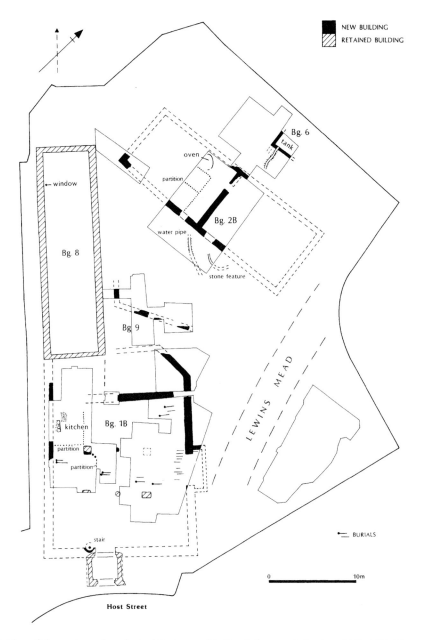

Fig. 5.4: Plan of the main archaeological features of St Bartholomew, Bristol, c. 1340–1400. The courtyard was maintained when the site underwent extensive rebuilding, with a new infirmary hall constructed against the north-west wall of Building 1B (the chapel). The area north of Building 2B remained a service area, although it appears that dormitory space was no longer utilised further north (Price & Ponsford 1998, 89, fig. 36. Reproduced with permission of the Council for British Archaeology © Roger Price, Michael Ponsford, and the Council for British Archaeology)

domestic waste that suggests people were living there. In the courtyard Building 9 replaced the path from Lewins Mead and may have served as a covered walk or series of rooms around the southern half of the courtyard and leading north alongside the eastern wall of Building 8, each section covered with a floor of coloured mortar and sand (Price & Ponsford 1998, 96–97). Building 2 was rebuilt on almost the same alignment and same configuration, but with side-by-side doors in the middle of the building leading into the room on the east and the central passageway that went through to the service area to the north (Price & Ponsford 1998, 97–101). Within this building in the western room were a cobbled kitchen floor, an oven, a set of drains to provide clean and remove dirty water, and soot and charcoal consistent with the activity of a kitchen, and to the east was a possible pantry or cupboard against the northern wall, and in the main room organic residues and multiple floor surfaces that led to the room being interpreted as the refectory. Fragments of statues were also found in the demolition, possibly suggesting some external decoration to the building or in the courtyard. To the north, Building 5 was replaced with Building 6, a structure seemingly rendered internally with mortar and clay, and with a conduit running down the western wall, suggesting this was a conduit house for the main water channel running from the Greyfriars to the north and which connected into the drainage system in Buildings 2, and 8, and possibly further south across the courtyard (Price & Ponsford 1998, 101–102). This period of construction and modification is associated with the hospital coming under the control of the lay sisters of the site, who set the hospital on a more financially stable footing, through actions like leasing the women's dormitory (Price & Ponsford 1998, 115–116). This may mean that the move to a single-story kitchen and refectory and the construction of an extension that seems to have served as an infirmary hall against the northwest wall of the chapel reflect a movement of the lay sisters and female inmates on site closer to the core of the site, perhaps in Building 8 now that the male staff members were removed or possibly staying above the chapel.

The fact that during this virtually complete rebuilding of the site, buildings remained in almost exactly the same pattern and were utilised for the same purposes as before does suggest that the nature of the site plan was not just functional but symbolically structured. Although the function of Building 9 is unclear, it did not survive long, being demolished and a covered claustral walk built around parts of the courtyard, possibly reflecting the return of administration to male masters in the 1380s under allegations of scandal and misadministration of the site by the lay sisters (Price & Ponsford 1998, 108). The only other domestic change after 1400, other than repairs to the floors of both the chapel and the kitchen refectory building, was that domestic waste was no longer found in the western half of the chapel and the partition removed. This possibly signifies the return to the pre-1340 layout, with staff either in the gallery of the chapel or in Building 8, one dormitory located either in the extension to the northwest of the chapel or in Building 8, and possibly the return to use of the women's dormitory to the north. The addition of the claustral walk and these domestic changes may have been influenced by the addition of the Fraternity of St Clement to the hospital between 1445 and 1490s. A group of 12 retired and invalided mariners who were given accommodation and a chapel in which to stay, and whom may have been housed in the northwestern addition to the chapel after the removal of the kitchen facilities (Price & Ponsford 1998, 120–121). Although the situation is far from clear about the living arrangements, the maintenance of two distinct spaces, one to the north of the chapel and likely associated with staff and perhaps male inmates, and the other to the north of the kitchen/refectory, comprising the other service buildings, probably the inmates' latrines, and the women's dormitory, is suggestive, especially as elements of this split can be seen at St Mary Spital.

St Mary, Ospringe

St Mary, at Ospringe in Kent, received royal patronage from its foundation during the mid-1230s and was constructed with a possible *Camera Regis*, an apartment for royal visitors travelling along Watling Street between Dover and Canterbury (Smith 1979, 82–86). This site saw very little development after its foundation, with only minor modification evident within the excavated area of the kitchen and the *camera*, and although there were a few buildings already on site, the layout of the hospital seems to have been constructed without obvious limits (Fig. 5.5). The infirmary hall, running north–south, and the chapel, running to the east in an L-shape, were not directly connected, but were separated by a short passageway or possibly the belfry for the chapel, as located by excavations in 2007 in the area between the chapel and the hall (Margetts 2011). The single-storey hall, comprising 8 bays and split into two halves by a north–south partition that communicated by a door at the northern end and possibly another to the south, was 36 m long with a culverted stream running north below the floor, likely housing between 30–40 inmates (Smith 1979, 91–93). To the northeast, entered via a doorway in the northern wall was what appears to be a latrine, although later erosion has destroyed most of the internal elements of the room. More drains entered the main stream from the east. To the west of the latrine, and against the northern wall of the infirmary the kitchen was constructed after the other buildings were complete, split into two rooms and which underwent multiple phases of modification to counter flooding in the hall (Smith 1979, 93). To the northwest of the infirmary hall, across a cobbled yard area, was Building 535, an east–west aligned rectangular building, not finished with ashlar trim like the hall and *camera*, with a hearth recessed into the southern wall and a drain through the northern wall of the east room, and a series of bases for ovens in the western room, leading to the interpretation of a bakehouse/brewhouse (Smith 1979, 96–97). West of this building was a storeroom, with the cemetery to the north, whilst to the south was the yard with a pond centrally located, and more buildings suggested by demolition material to the west of both the infirmary hall and the pond (Smith 1979, 98–99). The pond was surrounded by a wall and appears to have been regularly cleaned, suggesting an element of care about how this feature was utilised.

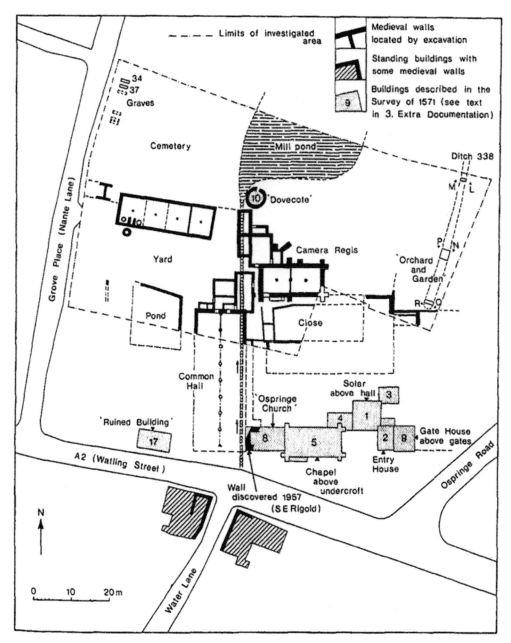

Fig. 5.5: Plan of the principal buildings at St Mary, Ospringe. The site appears split into two halves, the east associated with the religious community and the camera regis, the west with the infirmary and service buildings (Smith 1979, 85, fig. 2. Reproduced with permission of the Kent Archaeological Society)

To the northeast of the infirmary hall was the possible *camera* or high-status apartments, consisting of a main range with a public hall and private rooms leading off accessed via an external staircase, with an undercroft and a number of annexes, including a probable garderobe to the west and another undercroft room with a flint and chalk bench set against the western wall (Smith 1979, 99–101). Later a turret room with an internal staircase between the undercrofts and upper apartments was added to the *camera*, likely in the 14th century due to the use of diagonal buttresses. To the south was a garden close, with a wooden pentice on the western and southern side, possibly indicating a two-storey gallery that connected the *camera* with Building 415, of which only a small amount was within the excavation area, but which seems to have been a two-storey high-status building, possibly a staff refectory or guest quarters (Smith 1979, 101–102). Building 415 was constructed over an earlier 13th century well, suggesting some modification to this area of the site, between the chapel in the south and the *camera* in the north. To the east of Building 415 was another structure, with at least two wings, Buildings 1841 and 1842, although the majority of the structure was to the south, outside the excavation area (Smith 1979, 102). Building 1841 had a garderobe chute that was later blocked off, possibly in the 15th century since the construction was similar to other modifications at the north of the infirmary hall, indicating a shift from living quarters in the mid-15th century when the hospital experienced declining finances and support (Smith 1979, 102–103). A garden, irrigated by the regularly cleared out ditch that served the garderobe chute, was to the north of this building, possibly the same one noted in a 1401 *inspeximus* referring to the corrody paid by Sir Philip Wem for a chamber in a building close to the garden (Smith 1979, 103–104).

The plan at St Mary, Ospringe, clearly hinged along the join between the infirmary hall and the chapel, with the eastern half of the site hosting the chapel, the royal *camera*, the likely location of staff quarters, guest housing, gatehouse, and apartments for corrodians, whilst to the west was the infirmary hall, storerooms, bakehouse/ brewhouse, kitchen, and lay servants' accommodation (Smith 1979, 104–105). Both halves of the site also had their own courtyard and garden, and the culverted stream that served as the main drain appears to have been the line from which the two halves were separated. Another chapel, the lower chapel, was noted in documents from 1249–1250, but was likely in the unexcavated area to the southeast of the site, and may have either served the staff and high-status guests or was directly open to the road to service travellers. It should also be noted that virtually all of the site was constructed in one main phase at the point of foundation, allowing the greatest scope for establishing the desired layout, with a second phase of construction dating to the reign of Edward I, who funded refurbishments and additions in 1299 (Smith 1979, 105–106). As such, this site had the most scope of the three to set out its site as wished with the least limitations, and yet maintained a similar pattern, with the religious, male, and high-status area to the north and east of the chapel, and a secular, domestic, inmate area to the northwest and west of the chapel.

Deciphering complexity: intent, result, and hierarchies of space

By looking at the wider site a number of similarities in how space was divided up can be observed. There is a clear utilisation of courtyards or at least a series of ranges around an open area, some creating claustral systems, such as the canons cloister at St Mary Spital or the claustral walk between the *camera* and the possible staff quarters at St Mary, Ospringe, whilst others are less defined, such as the ranges around the Sisters' Garden at St Mary Spital, or the service area north of Building 2 at St Bartholomew's. Although the clear and regimented cloister of the monastery was not always directly implemented, activity areas were organised around an open space, corroborating the work of Gilchrist (1995) and Orme and Webster (1995). These spaces also remained surprisingly unchanging over the centuries, suggesting that this form served effectively in organising the daily lives of each community, associating certain spaces with specific groups of residents. These three case studies also indicate a clear wish to keep domestic activity and dormitory functions out of the chapel. Only at St Bartholomew's was an infirmary hall directly evident in the chapel after the initial construction phases, and this area was not only walled and partitioned off to clearly separate it from the rest of the chapel, it also appears to have been associated with the changes occurring in the period of management by the lay sisters, and disappeared when male masters were reinstated. This clearly argues against the necessity of the inmates' dormitory being directly linked to the chapel, although being close and having some access was important. At both St Mary Spital and St Bartholomew's the inmates had to walk outside to enter the chapel, in the case of St Mary Spital despite the fact the infirmary hall was attached to the chapel, possibly had windows between them, and had a communicating door blocked up, indicating this restriction of access was a conscious choice during the construction process. However, at each site an observable attempt to separate male and female inmates and staff does appear evident, whether in the two wards of the early phase of St Mary Spital or its later two-storey infirmary hall, the clear divide in the infirmary hall at St Mary, Ospringe, or in the construction of at least two dormitory areas for inmates at St Bartholomew's, one of which was specifically named the Women's Dormitory.

A pattern can be noted in the form of these sites that may reflect a conscious framework underpinning the English medieval hospitals. In all three cases the majority of buildings were located north of the chapel, arguably due to the constraints of the landscape and land ownership, although it is debatable if this was a crucial issue at all but St Bartholomew's. However, all three sites located the religious men in the closest buildings, just north of the chapel, with other buildings radiating out to the northwest. This created a hierarchy of space, with the eastern side of the site serving as the religious male area, and where the hosting of high-status guests was also carried out. To the west, the secular and domestic area was located, focussed upon the maintenance of the entire community, but specifically the inmates. Further northwest, where a clear female staff presence was noted, were located the women, furthest from the chapel and religious men. When the Sisters were brought closer to the chapel area at St Mary Spital a clear separation between the women and inmates and the area of the canons was first established by an arcade between the Sisters' Garden and the Kitchen Garden and then later monumentalised by the addition of a closed off passageway between the Sisters' Refectory and a kitchen serving window. What is unclear is why the dormitories and wider claustral arrangements of the religious men were not located to the south of the chapel in any of these cases, especially at St Mary Spital and St Mary, Ospringe, where space or the nature of the site formation could have allowed a different layout. On the limited evidence of these three sites, it could be argued that this location to the north was intentional, possibly highlighting the non-monastic nature of the community whilst still organising the site as a quasi-monastic form by flipping the traditional monastic layout to the north. The highest status building, the chapel, served as the orientation point at the southeast of the complex, from which the site was structured. This indicates a similar architectural development between all the sites, a planned spatial framework that was modified by each site's own biography of construction.

These case studies indicate an *intent* towards a hierarchy of space that was clearly east to west, a usual trend in Christian buildings, but also for a hierarchy from southeast to northwest, something less (if at all) discussed. The kitchens also seemed to serve as liminal points between the two areas, located in the middle of each site and serving, at least in the case of St Mary Spital and St Bartholomew's, both spheres. This likely does relate to functional common sense, but given the importance of food to the function of the hospital, there may also be a symbolic undertone. There are also clear courtyard and garden spaces associated with each sphere, potential locations for separated light exercise and contemplation for each part of the community, and coupled with the vital role of the chapel and the organised space it can be argued that rather than purely organic constructions there was an *intent* for a planned religious layout, with the specific *results* moulded or changed for the individual biographies of each site. This hypothesised framework was not one that led to strictly identical physical layouts, but one where a few key elements or *intents*, such as spatial orientations, hierarchies of space, and the association of specific parts of the site with sections of the community that reflected the nature of the charitable work carried out, the creation of a healing and restorative religious environment, and the clear establishment of a place of pious good work, was still evident in the *results* of the varied building forms, the phases of rebuilding or modification, and the different sizes of each community. Here can be seen enough of a similarity for this rather disparate collection of institutions to be united under the term 'hospital', a visible and understandable architectural layout to charity, faith, and medicine. Such a form is only evident when the site is seen as a complex of buildings and associations, where choices were made to follow the *intent* of the framework but for which the *result* was not always the same exact layout, direct association, or shape. Indeed, the choices reflecting these *intents* and *results* need not have always been fully understood or appreciated by those inhabiting, administering, building, or founding the sites.

This theoretical model needs to be tested more widely against the full range of English hospital architecture, including St Giles, Brompton Bridge (Cardwell 1995), St Mary Magdalen, Partney (Atkins & Popescu 2010), and St John the Baptist, Oxford (Durham 1991), but it serves as a starting point. From this framework, a more grounded debate can occur over the differences observed between hospitals sites, how distinctive regionality may be (for example the possibility of a distinctly Kentish layout of L- and T-shaped hospitals; see Gilchrist 1995; Margetts 2011; Prescott 1992), and how the needs of the different communities may have affected the relationship between the infirmary hall and the chapel. The concepts of *intent* and *result* also allow us to interrogate the physical remains and contextualise the individual site biographies that have frequently hindered wider discussion. It is unclear whether the northern association holds a more ideological or symbolic message, although the north in Christian religious buildings has been connected to women, the moon, cold, and the Old Testament, as well as the Virgin Mary being at the right hand of Christ during the Crucifixion, which on the medieval rood screen would place her north of the altar (Gilchrist 1994, 133–135). When discussing later medieval nunneries Gilchrist (1994, 136–138, 148–149) suggested it may also represent an association with, or emulation of, some of the refounded Anglo-Saxon double monasteries, where men and women lived on the same site and the women's cloister was located to the north in a duality with the location of men to the south. This emulation of Anglo-Saxon monasticism and mixed houses may also have been used to set apart the hospital, linking the institution back to some of its founding principles in early alms practices. It would also have served as a plan for the negotiation of gendered, or more specifically female, space with men, and in particular monastic men, a source of difficulty, contention and difference. By referencing Mary, and her obvious centrality to such redemptive portions of Jesus' life as his birth, death, and resurrection, as well as her own life, death, and elevation, all of which would have been positive contemplative stories in the hospital environment, it may also have provided added religious significance and support for those residing with the hospital complex. Unfortunately, the specific ideological underpinning of this framework is not yet clear, but the fact that this northern association was not just functional but symbolic and may not just be limited to hospitals but also nunneries may have important implications for other non-monastic institutions, such as friaries, military orders, or secular colleges.

To conclude, the three case studies of St Mary Spital, St Bartholomew, and St Mary, Ospringe, suggest a framework in which the hospital, just like nunneries or any other religious institution, should be treated as a complex, where the hierarchy of space and a northern orientation need not be functional or due to restrictions of space, but an intentional ideological choice. The form reflected the purposeful *result* of the *intent* to organise a religious and healing environment for those admitted to benefit from the charitable care provided, highlighting the quasi-monastic nature of the inhabitants. That this care was often corrupt, impoverished, or carried out in buildings with structural failings only reflects that the *result* need not match the *intent*.

This framework helps engage with the seemingly disparate material in a manner that both ties into the nature of these sites and the intended care they were designed to carry out. It is only after there is an understanding of what threads unified these sites that the differences can begin to be unpicked.

Bibliography

Agrimi, J. & Crisciani, C. (1998) Charity and aid in medieval Christian civilization. In M. Grmek (ed.) *Western Medical Thought from Antiquity to the Middle Ages*, translated by A. Shugaar, 170–196. London, Harvard University Press.

Atkins, R. & Popescu, E. (2010) Excavations at the Hospital of St Mary Magdalen, Partney, Lincolnshire, 2003. *Medieval Archaeology* 54, 204–270.

Bourdieu, P. (1970) The Berber house of the world reversed. *Social Science Information* 9 (2), 151–170.

Buklijaš, T. (2008) Medicine and society in the medieval hospital. *Croatian Medical Journal* 49, 151–154.

Cardwell, P. (1995) Excavation at the hospital of St Giles by Brompton Bridge, North Yorkshire. *The Archaeological Journal* 152, 109–245.

Carlin, M. (1989) Medieval English hospitals. In L. Granshaw & R. Porter (eds.) *The Hospital in History*, 21–39. London, Routledge.

Clay, M. R. (1909) *The Medieval Hospitals of England*. London, Methuen.

Connell, B., Jones, A. G., Redfern, R. & Walker, D. (2012) *A Bioarchaeological Study of Medieval Burials on the Site of St Mary Spital: Excavations at Spitalfields Market, London E1, 1991–2007*. Museum of London Archaeological Services Monograph 60. London, Museum of London Archaeology.

Dainton, C. (1976) Medieval hospitals of England. *History Today* 26 (8), 532–538.

Davis, A. (2010) Preaching in thirteenth-century hospitals. *Journal of Medieval History* 36 (1), 72–89.

Durham, B. (1991) The infirmary and hall of the medieval hospital of St John the Baptist at Oxford. *Oxoniensia* 56, 17–75.

Egan, G. (2007) Material culture of care for the sick: some excavated evidence from English medieval hospitals and other sites. In B. Bower (ed.) *The Medieval Hospital and Medical Practice*, 65–76. Aldershot, Ashcroft

Gilchrist, R. (1992) Christian bodies and souls: the archaeology of life and death in later medieval hospitals. In S. Bassett (ed.) *Death in Towns: Urban Responses to the Dying and the Dead, 100–1600*, 101–118. London, Leicester University Press.

Gilchrist, R. (1994) *Gender and Material Culture: The Archaeology of Religious Women*. Abingdon, Routledge.

Gilchrist, R. (1995) *Contemplation and Action: The Other Monasticism*. London, Leicester University Press.

Gilchrist, R. & Sloane, B. (2005) *Requiem: The Medieval Monastic Cemetery in Britain*. London, Museum of London Archaeological Service.

Godfrey, W. (1955) *The English Almshouse: With Some Account of its Predecessor the Medieval Hospital*. London, Faber.

Horden, P. (2001) Religion as medicine: Music in medieval hospitals. In P. Biller & J. Ziegler (eds.) *Religion and Medicine in the Middle Ages*, York Studies in Medieval Theology III, 135–153. York, York Medieval Press.

Horden, P. (2007) A non-natural environment: medicine without doctors and the medieval European hospital. In B. Bower (ed.) *The Medieval Hospital and Medical Practice*, 133–145. Aldershot, Ashcroft.

Krautheimer, R. (1942) Introduction to an 'iconography of mediaeval architecture'. *Journal of the Warburg and Courtauld Institutes* 5, 1–33.

Leistikow, D. (1967) *Ten Centuries of European Hospital Architecture: A Contribution to the History of Hospital Architecture*. Ingelheim and Rhein, C. H. Boehringer Sohn.

Margetts, A. (2011) The medieval hospital of St Mary the Blessed Virgin, Ospringe (*Maison Dieu*): Further details of its original layout revealed by excavations at the Fairways. *Archaeologia Cantiana* 131, 129–142.

McIntosh, M. (2012) *Poor Relief in England, 1350–1600.* Cambridge, Cambridge University Press.

Melhuish, C. (2005) Towards a phenomenology of a concrete megastructure: Space and perception at the Brunswick Centre, London. *Journal of Material Culture* 10 (1), 5–29.

Orme, N. & Webster, M. (1995) *The English Hospital, 1070–1570.* London, Yale University Press.

Parker Pearson, M. & Richards, C. (1994) Ordering the world: perceptions of architecture, space and time. In M. Parker Pearson & C. Richards (eds) *Architecture and Order: Approaches to Social Space*, 1–37. London, Routledge.

Prescott, E. (1992) *The English Medieval Hospital, 1050–1640.* London, Seaby.

Price, R. & Ponsford, M. (1998) *St Bartholomew's Hospital Bristol. The Excavations of a Medieval Hospital: 1976-8.* Council for British Archaeology Research Report 110. York, Council for British Archaeology.

Rawcliffe, C. (1984) The hospitals later medieval London. *Medical History* 28, 1–21.

Rawcliffe, C. (1995) *Medicine and Society in Later Medieval England.* Stroud, Sutton.

Rawcliffe, C. (1999) *Medicine for the Soul: The Life, Death and Resurrection of an English Medieval Hospital.* Stroud, Sutton.

Rawcliffe, C. (2006) *Leprosy in Medieval England.* Woodbridge, Boydell Press.

Roberts, J. (2007) An Investigation of Medieval Hospitals in England, Scotland, and Wales 1066–1560. PhD diss., University of Wales, Newport.

Roffey, S. (2012) Medieval leper hospitals in England: An archaeological perspective. *Medieval Archaeology* 56, 203–233.

Rowe, J. (1958) The medieval hospitals of Bury St. Edmunds. *Medieval History* 2 (4), 253–263.

Rubin, M. (1989) Development and change in English hospitals, 1100–1500. In L. Granshaw & R. Porter (eds.) *The Hospital in History*, 41–59. London, Routledge.

Smith, G. H. (1979) The excavation of the Hospital of St Mary of Ospringe, commonly called Maison Dieu. *Archaeologia Cantiana* 95, 81–184.

Sotres, P. (1998) The regimens of health. In M. Grmek (ed.) *Western Medical Thought from Antiquity to the Middle Ages*, translated by Anthony Shugaar, 291–318. London, Harvard University Press.

Sweetinburgh, S. (2004) *The Roles of the Hospital in Medieval England: Gift-giving and the Spiritual Economy.* Dublin, Four Courts Press.

Thomas, C., Sloane, B. & Phillpotts, C. (1997) *Excavations at the Priory and Hospital of St Mary Spital, London.* Museum of London Archaeological Services Monograph 1. London, Museum of London Archaeological Services.

Watson, S. (2006) The origins of the English hospital. *Transactions of the Royal Historical Society* 16, 75–94.

Part 2

Central and Eastern Europe

Chapter 6

A house within the settlement: Early Byzantine 'urban life' in a small-scale house?

Miriam Steinborn

'*Der Mensch ist mit seinem Wohnorte so nah verwandt, daß die Betrachtung über diesen uns auch über seinen Bewohner aufklären muß.*'

'Man is so closely related to his domicile, that the examination of it has to enlighten us about its inhabitants.'

J. W. Goethe, Letter to Carl von Knebel, 30. 12. 1785 (Goethe 1891, No. 2230)

As a researcher, Goethe stated an archaeological principle: the close connection between people and their dwellings makes it possible to draw conclusions about the inhabitants by taking a look at their houses. But houses are more: they are the physical environment in which household takes place. 'Household' is a complex concept that involves the physical layout, the people involved and their everyday life, their social relations and their economic practices. In its variety it has been the object of debated definitions (see Deetz 1982, 717–718; Wilk & Rathje 1982, 618, 621, 631–633; Hendon 1996, 47; Bernbeck 1997, 185–187; Netting 2002, 58; Anderson 2004, 109–112; Bonine 2004, 15–17 amongst others). In the 1980s the idea of household became a unit of archaeological investigation, at least since the constitutive article of Wilk and Rathje (1982). They defined household on a social and material level, and also by behaviour concerning the domestic strategy to secure continuation. This strategy contains four categories of function: production, distribution, reproduction and transmission. This functionalistic approach may not cover each aspect of everyday life that takes place in households, but it contextualises the archaeological finds with the social system and the physical settlement system. This paper approaches the understanding of the city context with the investigation of economic and social practices. These categories will be applied in a microstudy on the material of a small-scale house in Caričin Grad.

Building 23 in Caričin Grad

The early Byzantine settlement of Caričin Grad in southern Serbia is thought to be the imperial city Iustiniana Prima and was inhabited for merely 90 years in the 6th and 7th century AD (Ivanišević 2016a, 109, 124–126). Since there aren't any settlement remains dating after this period, the excavations provide undisturbed insights into the development of early Byzantine urban life. One goal of the German project titled 'The short life of an imperial city – daily life, environment and fall of the early Byzantine city Caričin Grad (Iustiniana Prima?)' undertaken from 2014 to 2017 at the Römisch Germanisches Zentralmuseum Mainz was to gain information about the social and economic basis of everyday life in this settlement. Therefore Building 23, hereinafter abbreviated as B23, was excavated with consideration of the concept and methodology of household archaeology. The following conclusions are based on the preliminary results.

B23 is an example of modest architecture in the upper town of Caričin Grad and shares constructional similarities with other elementary buildings in the settlement. It was a semi-detached house with a single room of four to six meters with a masonry base and walls made of adobe and presumably an intermediate floor or an attic storey, as indicated by remains of charred planks. The facade of B23 was orientated towards the street, running along close to the house in the north, where an 80 cm wide doorway allowed direct access to the room (Fig. 6.1). An absolute age determination based on finds is not possible, since the only coin, a follis minted between AD 512 and 538, can't be used for dating because it is originated from the debris layer. It provides only a *terminus post quem* that dates the destruction of the house after the time of the foundation of the city – a quite obvious observation. Nevertheless the stratigraphic sequence of the buildings revealed the relative chronology of B23 and it was inserted into a developed urban structure of the northern town quarter (Fig. 6.2). The house walls were attached to a tower of the inner fortification wall belonging to the Acropolis, which is regarded as part of the initial phase of the city (Ivanišević 2016a, 109, 111). A drainage system dug into the bedrock dewatered the rainfall from the roof of the tower into the underground of a street. B23 was built upon this free area in front of the tower and above the drainage, so the further use of the system was inhibited. A compensating canal was built between the house and its neighbouring structure. The ground-plan of the house and the fortification tower determine the roof construction as a pent-roof with a pediment to the west, so rain would be drained from the tower and the roof onto the street.

The modest architecture of B23, and few objects discovered through excavation connected with specific activities, broaden the range of potential activities that may have been conducted there. Houses with several rooms provide the possibility of specialisation in spatial use and its expression in fixed installations; in contrast a small single room structure was necessarily used in a multifunctional way, potentially also involving removable, flexible solutions. An irrefutable interpretation is therefore restricted. B23 contained two fixed installations, the remains of a fireplace and

Fig. 6.1: B23, activity zones after Sommer 1990

fragments of at least one pithos that indicate storage facilities (Fig. 6.1) belonging to the occupation phase. This suggests a habitational function, which is supported by rather domestic ceramic material. The excavation didn't reveal any hints that the structure underwent more than one phase of use as house, and it is impossible to track short time changeovers of occupants if they didn't change archaeological visible features.

The concept of household

A house and a conjugated household are not necessarily equivalent, as the question of spatial use will point out below. To work on households always means working

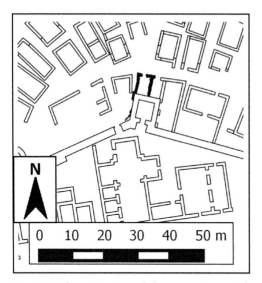

Fig. 6.2: Urban structure of the upper town with Acropolis and neighbouring houses of B23, Caričin Grad

with an abstract concept; therefore, a specification of the idea is required. In this study, the household is defined as a bundle of activities if the domestic strategy following Wilk and Rathje (1982), conducted by a group of persons using the space of B23. The activities cover at least feeding and most likely sleeping, which is difficult to trace archaeologically, especially if it did not take place on the ground floor and involved since decayed bed constructions. Since the finds do not allow judgement of whom and how many people belonged to the group, it is possible that it consists of only one single person or more, also in changing composition.

Households imply a material component, and one should be reminded that archaeologists excavate house-structures and not households (Wilk & Rathje 1982, 619). The recovered material culture is not the direct evidence of activities within the structures but rather the reflection of activities conducted within the household context (Hendon 2004, 275–276). Careful examinations of houses and households have to consider cultural formation processes. Cleaning and waste removal change finds assemblages, as do practices like legacy or trade. During the abandonment of towns, the inhabitants decide whether to take or leave objects at the property. The remaining objects are in most cases regarded as worthless or waste. A careful analysis of formations processes also works as middle range theory on a material-based level (Smith 2011, 168–173). To gain insights into the organisation of work it is necessary to examine the activities in- and outside the building. Thus it is possible to understand the agency households perform in settlement systems regarding social, religious and economic aspects.

The conjunction of data and concept – activity areas

Wilk and Rathje (1982) defined the domestic strategy of a household by the four categories of function: production, distribution, reproduction and transmission. The approach builds a bridge between the empirical data and an abstract system and can be applied as middle range theory, as defined by Merton (2007, 452). Production comprises everything that is generated within the household context, including processing of purchased raw material, which means the production and procession of food, but also every-day goods such as textiles (Wilk & Rathje 1982, 622–624). It is impossible to define precisely the boundary between household production and handicraft, and it is even more difficult if a workshop is inserted into the architectural layout of the dwelling space. Furthermore, the income generated from this economic sphere cannot be seen separately from the budget of the household. The topic of production is often well studied, also without referring to the household itself, since it is regarded as fundamental to a working town system and it has the potential to leave archaeological visible traces.

Production in B23

The arrangement of the door, fireplace, and storage area guides the spatial organisation of movement and activities (Fig. 6.1). The northern part of the small house provided light and warmth; in winter supplied by the simply constructed fireplace and in summer by opening the door to the street allowing in daylight. There are no remains of lamps or other artificial light sources amongst the finds of the occupational phase in B23. Leaving aside the possibilities that the contrivances could have been taken away or did not leave traces, this suggests the occupants were mainly dependent on the fireplace and natural light. It could have been provided by small windows, since fragments of glass occurred in the features belonging to the decayed walls of B23. The windows would have been inserted into the western or the northern wall on the ground-floor or into the gable to the west. The light could have reached the ground floor, but also light the intermediate floor or an attic storey – an argument based on a chain of circumstantial evidences. The bright area on the ground floor is rather small, despite this, light-dependent activities, whether handcraft or household chore, had to take place here. The excavation did not reveal material expressions of activities, however this is the expected outcome of a multifunctional space as it had to be kept clean. The fireplace also provided the possibility to cook. The storage area was situated at the middle of the western wall face to face with the fireplace. Usually *pithoi* have been at least partly dug into the ground, therefore it is very possible that the storage container was originally placed there and not much moved after the abandonment of the house. The spatial layout reduced the opportunity to move in the small rectangular room that was not further divided by partitions, but the installation of curtains could have been used to structure the space additionally. Entrants had to turn slightly to the left, and thus the small corner right-hand of the entrance became a peripheral passive area, possibly a place to deposit things (Sommer 1990, 52–53). The back site of the room in the south at the wall of the tower did not reveal any hints of its use. It is peculiar that the storage vessel was not placed here which would have provided more space at the entrance and in the middle of the room. One solution to this unusual arrangement could be the physical character of the place regarding aspects of temperature and moisture that would affect the items in stock. Indeed the excavation revealed a damper area in the southeastern corner, above the former construction ditch of the towers foundation. It is of course possible that the humidity was the result of centuries of decay, since the missing roof of the modern reconstruction of the tower created something akin to a leaky basin. This was evident during the excavation as rainwater permeated under the tower into the excavation trench. It is possible, but of course not inevitably true, that processes like this did also occur in the utilisation phase of B23. The floor in this area was covered with mainly homogenous loam material that might have been applied to counter the damp. The southwestern corner of the room was dryer but could not be used to dig in a storage vessel, because the cover of the precedent canal created a shallow floor level.

It was impractical to extend the domestic activity zone on a footway outside the door, since the street was almost directly adjacent. The only opportunity to spread the activity area was to move to a remote working space, both inside other houses or outdoors. Spatial outsourced workshops, such as gardens, fields, courtyards, or other shared spaces in squares and public infrastructure, distributed over the settlement can be part of the spatial organisation of everyday life (Anderson 2004, 117–120). It is difficult to link these spaces to separate house structures and with that to individual households. Furthermore, activities within one household can be separated among several houses (Bernbeck 1997, 185–187). Therefore it is always possible that the excavated house structures do not contain the whole range of household chores, especially if they provided only limited space.

The objects of B23 are rather elementary. Some iron objects have not yet been categorised, however they seem to belong to a context of craftsmanship. Since there are no further archaeological traces of a workshop there are two possible explanations. The crafter could have worked very neatly so there are no archaeological remains of his work. Conversely, he could have kept some tools at home, while working at another place. A reaping hook found in B23 (Fig. 6.3) was used in an agrarian context; the shape of the tool with a long blade and a curved end was presumably primarily used for crop harvesting. In contrast to fully curved sickles that allowed constant swinging and fast movement, the reaping hook requires one hand on the tool and the other on the stems. It makes the process slower, but the whole operation of cutting and collecting is in one step of the procedure and involves one person. Therefore this instrument suits smaller plots and tasks connected to environments like gardens or shrubbery. This indicates a self-sufficient economy that allows the household to produce its own food to a certain extent. The evidence of craftsmanship and agriculture within the household context illustrate that important daily tasks did not take place within the ground plan of B23; however the building contributed significantly to the everyday life of the people who used it.

There are several knives in the assemblage (Fig. 6.3), but their actual use is difficult to specify, since the shape of the blades do not have functional significance (Manning 1986, 108). Both blades with tangs may have belonged to knives used in general purposes, however the knife with the twisted handle differs from them. It was not suitable for lever movements, unless it was equipped with a stabilising organic handle that would have covered the twisted decoration. It may have been used for cutting weak material or for a spreading application of pastes presumably in a cooking context.

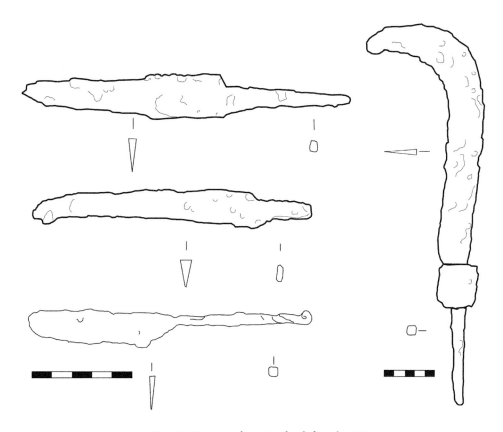

Fig. 6.3: Knives and reaping hook found in B23

The finds of B23 are connected with production in handcraft and rural economy; tasks that are deeply connected with the male-centric work, following the 4th-century bishop Johannes Chrysostomos (PG 51.230; Clark 1993, 100–101). He declared that women should work in private and not in public, and that they are better in doing housework, raising children and working on textiles. Consequential, there are no finds of textile production or related crafts in B23 and therefore no evidence of typical 'female' work, as defined by Chrysostomos, except for the knives that may have been kitchen equipment however these of course could be assigned to a single male. The issue of attitudes towards social gender and biological sex is a topic for itself and it is often an oversimplification to assign labour to male or female parts. On the one hand there is the methodological difficulty of archaeological evidence and on the other hand there is a hermeneutic problem that is a dichotomous classification of work might reflect modern gender attitudes (Sénécheau 2014, 70–83). Written sources could help to understand, but be misleading also, since they can display an idealistic world view, especially when it comes to the fathers of the church. The misogyny of Chrysostomos is known (Galatariotou 1984, 49–93), at least are his efforts to emphasise women's place at home. Ideal habitual orientations may not include the real life of less privileged women who had to work as female agrarian activities scarcely appear explicitly in the written sources (Laiou 1981, 248–249). One exception is the pagan philosopher Hierocles who described farming and harvesting by women (Stobaeus 4, 29; Clark 1993, 101). Unfortunately they can't be linked to tools evidently. The only solution to this lack of assurance is further anthropologic research to gain information of pathological changes (Alt & Röder 2014, 202–209; Gerstel 2015, 93–95).

The actions in the attic storey are once again problematic. Observations on well preserved late-antique rural houses in Syria and Cilicia show that the ground floor was used as storage area and barns in most cases, while the upper storey served as a dwelling area (Eichner 2011, 460–474). This functional division was also observed in the urban shops of Sardis (Crawford 1990, 108) and known from written sources concerning Constantinople (Janin 1950, 91–100), with further examples dating to traditional Roman patterns of use. It is very likely that this division of space did also occur in Caričin Grad, but there is little evidence from the excavation to support this. Life in the attic took place above the ground, and furnishing in Roman tradition was sparse and often comprised organic material (Russel 2000, 80; Papanikola-Bakirtzi 2013, 219–222). There is only one find connected with dwelling within B23: clumsily carved fragments of a bone mount may have been applied on an element of furniture - maybe a small chest. The spread distribution of the fragments indicates that it could have been in the attic when it collapsed.

Distribution in B23

The domestic production is interlinked with distribution, which covers all transitional aspects between production and consumption. It involves several activities like gathering, storing and providing resources for consumption and production, but also the exchange of goods. Larger households often provided a greater variety and quality of homemade products, thus requiring extensive storage facilities. Smaller households conducted a limited production and as a result distribution was less comprehensive (Wilk & Rathje 1982, 624–627). B23 provided only limited space and was equipped with only one archaeologically detectable storage vessel. The small stock indicates a minor household, even if it was supplemented with smaller ceramic or organic containers like pots and baskets. It is likely, that B23 contained only the most important goods for immediate use while other items were stored elsewhere. Possible scenarios are for example a joint property situated in the neighbouring house or exchange at the marketplace.

Invisible functions? Reproduction and transmission in B23

The other two functions of domestic strategies are not as archaeologically visible as production or distribution might be; in fact, reproduction is much more virtual.

The biological and mental reproduction of people consolidates social and economic structures of the town. Prevalent uncodified social rules regulated the cohabitation and collaboration in the limited space of the house and the city. Bourdieu (2009) revealed how daily routines shaped the domestic setting and work as mechanisms of socialisation. The household can be seen as the place where social roles are negotiated in daily routine and therefore reproduced. The finds are not chronologically sensitive enough to draw conclusions about the life span of B23; it is not clear weather parents and children or single persons used it. However it is possible that the house sheltered at least two generations reproducing the social system and the biological group while keeping the house, living and working together.

Transmission means the intergenerational transfer of rights, functions, land and goods and is therefore a special type of reproduction and distribution (Wilk & Rathje 1982, 627–630). It is difficult to trace transmission in archaeological context, however should be considered as it potentially affects the archaeological find assemblage. The opportunity to bequest objects depends on the prevalent concept of ownership and it is possible to conclude from testaments which objects may have been bequeathed. The legislative digests of Corpus Iuris Civilis show that indefeasible facilities are objects that are imperative for the use of the building; for example, vessels in taverns, mills in bakeries or manpower in rural estates and so on (CICiv Dig. 33,7). Household effects, including food and movable inanimate goods do not belong to this category, rather they can be part of transfer agreements. Likewise, personal belongings like gold, silver, clothing and individual property are a further separate category. Therefore, leaving a house means transferring all household effects except personal and intrinsic items. In B23 the only transferable object was the storage vessel. It is possible that it was left because it belonged to the inventory of the building. However there is also a second explanation for this: although it was quite expensive (Giannopoulou 2010, 33–36) it was also heavy and big, and it is possible that the effort to pack and transport it to a new dwelling space was more than the expenditure to get a new one (Sommer 1990, 53–58).

The social sphere – who lived in B23?

The finds can be used to reduce the possible variations of group members. If it was a single person household, it consisted at least for a certain time most likely of a male person, since the crafting tools are thought to be more commonly used by men. There are no indications that the single person had a relationship or not, familial or professional, with the neighbouring household. If the group consisted of more than one person, the possibility of variation increases; possible examples could be a celibate co-residence in a Christian context or a nuclear family (Clark 1993, 100–101). Historical research indicates that the importance of marriage and parenthood increased in the 6th century (Rautman 2006, 39–60; Laiou 2009, 51–52). The finds do not depict explicitly the presence of children or women, however this does not disprove their existence. A zoomorphic antler attachment created as a pig's head could have been part of a toy, but it is also possible that it adorned an object used by adults. A few unornamented buckles are all that remained from personal jewellery and they do not reveal much about the wearer. Some simple beads cut from bone are also rather unspecific and could have been applied to clothes as well as to furnishing objects. Despite the limited positive evidences, the finds demonstrate one aspect: they do not appear to have been owned by wealthy or high-status people. This impression is underlined by the elementary design of the architecture and the economic choice of building material. B23 accommodated one or more persons who belonged to an average or low social stratum. Goods were generated through two strategies if indeed the evidence belongs to the same occupants. The household was engaged in agriculture and/or horticulture, but economic income was also gained with handcraft. If both strategies took place at the same time, the chances increase that the household consisted of more than one person.

The context of B23 – household and settlement

The domestic activities display in part the organisation of the whole settlement. In the 6th- and 7th-century Byzantine settlements underwent a transformation, starting from their late antique roots to their middle Byzantine character. The layout of Caričin Grad demonstrates classic Roman influences, such as a secular administration building, thermae and an aqueduct, and new elements like a fortified ecclesiastical area on the highest place (Bouras 1981, 642–650).

Distribution strategies on the household level indicate the economic strategy of the settlement (Wilk & Rathje 1982, 627). Following Wilk and Rathje (1982), households in urban contexts tend to exchange goods, while in rural contexts pooling is of greater importance. The evidence of private storage facilities, especially if observed regularly, may therefore suggest a rather rural economy. This impression is supported by the agrarian tool in B23. Autarchy was a major economic aspect (Baron, Reuter & Markovic 2018) in the 6th century, as indicated by frequent finds of agricultural tools and zoological and botanical remains in city contexts – it is also reflected in historic reports. Theophylactus Simocatta described a raid in AD 584, when numerous inhabitants of Singidunum were overtaken by Avars during the harvest outside the walls (Theophylactus Simocatta, hist. 1, 3-4; Ivanišević 2016b, 93). A similar episode was reported in the Miracles of St Demetrius, concerning a Slavic attack on Thessaloniki (Miracula Sancti Demetrii 2, § 199; Milinković 2007, 179–182). The inhabitants of the settlement arranged their lives themselves. The agriculture, private storing strategy and waste disposal are echoes of this way of living. The distribution of finds shows that B23 was basically kept clean, in contrast to the streets that were, at least at the end of the settlement activity, filled with waste items. The 'Life of Symeon Salos' (BHG 1677) reports rubbish heaps outside the city walls of Emesa in the 6th century (Saradi 2014, 424), indicating a communal organisation. Waste accumulating in the street could be the result of a weak administration. The architectural change of the fortification wall that lost its strategical function through extensions like B23 suggests the same, because it wasn't prevented efficiently. Lifestyle changed from a consuming to a productive subsistence – or rather from an urban to a rural character. The finds are too unspecific to define the everyday life in this particular house. However analysing them with methodologies of household archaeology like the categories of function by Wilk and Rathje (1982) generates detailed questions about average people that are not asked from a broader approach to the settlement. The seemingly minor insights into everyday life in B23 from an economic and social perspective grant access to the wider context in which it was set – the early Byzantine city of Caričin Grad.

Bibliography

Alt, K. W. & Röder, B. (2014) Der inkorporierte Alltag: Sterbliche Überreste als Zugang zur prähistorischen Geschlechter- und Kindheitsgeschichte. In B. Röder (ed.) *Ich Mann. Du Frau: Feste Rollen seit Urzeiten?*, 202–209. Berlin, Rombach.

Anderson, N. (2004) Finding space between spatial boundaries and social dynamics: The archaeology of nested households. In K. S. Barile and J. C. Brandon (eds.) *Household Chores and Household Choices: Theorizing the Domestic Sphere in Historical Archaeology*, 109–120. Tuscaloosa, University of Alabama Press.

Baron, H., Reuter, A. & Markovic, N. (2018) Rethinking ruralization in terms of resilience: Subsistence strategies in sixth-century Caričin Grad in the light of plant and animal bone finds. *Quaternary International* (online: doi: 10.1016/j.quaint.2018.02.031).

Bernbeck, R. (1997) *Theorien in der Archäologie*. Tübingen, Francke.

Bonine, M. (2004) Analysis of household and family at a Spanish colonial rancho along the Rio Grande. In K. S. Barile & J. C. Brandon (eds.) *Household Chores and Household Choices: Theorizing the Domestic Sphere in Historical Archaeology*, 15–32. Tuscaloosa, University of Alabama Press.

Bouras, C. (1981) City and village: Urban design and architecture. *Jahrbuch der österreichischen Byzantinistik* 31 (2), 611–653.

Bourdieu, P. (2009) *Entwurf einer Theorie der Praxis auf der ethnologischen Grundlage der kabylischen Gesellschaft*. 2nd ed. Frankfurt am Main, Suhrkamp.

Clark, G. (1994) *Women in Late Antiquity: Pagan and Christian Life-Styles*. Oxford, Oxford University Press.

Crawford, J. S. (1990) *The Byzantine Shops at Sardis*. Monograph / Archaeological Exploration of Sardis 9. Cambridge, Harvard University Press.

Deetz, J. J. F. (1982) Households: A structural key to archaeological explanation. *American Behavioural Scientist* 25 (6), 717–724.

Eichner, I. (2011) *Frühbyzantinische Wohnhäuser in Kilikien: Baugeschichtliche Untersuchung zu den Wohnformen in der Region um Seleukeia am Kalykadnos*. Istanbuler Forschungen 52. Tübingen, E. Wasmuth.

Galatariotou, C. S. (1984) Holy women and witches: Aspects of Byzantine conceptions of gender. *Byzantine and Modern Greek Studies* 9 (1), 55–94.

Gerstel, S. E. (2015) *Rural Lives and Landscapes in Late Byzantium*. Cambridge, Cambridge University Press.

Giannopoulou, M. (2010) *Pithoi: Technology and History of Storage Vessels through the Ages*. British Archaeological Reports International Series 2140. Oxford, Archaeopress.

Goethe, J. W. von (1891) *Goethes Werke, Abteilung 4 Briefe, Band 7 Weimar: 1. Januar 1785 - 24. Juli 1786*. Weimar, Böhlau.

Hendon, J. A. (1996) Archaeological approaches to the organization of domestic labour: Household practice and domestic relations. *Annual Review of Anthropology* 25 (1), 45–61.

Hendon, J. A. (2004) Living and working at home: The social archaeology of household production and social relations. In L. Meskell & R. W. Preucel (eds.) *A Companion to Social Archaeology*, 272–285. Malden, Blackwell.

Ivanišević, V. (2016a) Caričin Grad (Justiniana Prima): A new-discovered city for a 'new' society. In S. Marjanović-Dušanić (ed.) *Proceedings of the 23rd International Congress of Byzantine Studies, Belgrade, 22-27 August 2016: Plenary Papers*, 107–126. Belgrade, Serbian National Committee of Association Internationale des Etudes Byzantines.

Ivanišević, V. (2016b) Late antique cities and their environment in northern Illyricum. In F. Daim & J. Drauschke (eds.) *Hinter den Mauern und auf dem offenen Land: Leben im Byzantinischen Reich, Byzanz zwischen Orient und Okzident 3*, 89–99. Mainz, Verlag des Römisch-Germanischen Zentralmuseums.

Janin, R. (1950) *Constantinople - Byzantine: Développement Urbain et Répertoire Topographique*. Archives de l'Orient Chrétien 4 A. Paris, Institut Français d'Etudes Byzantines.

Knütel, R., Krampe, C. & Behrends, O. (eds.) (2012) *Corpus iuris civilis 5. Digesten 28 - 34: Text und Übersetzung*. Heidelberg, C. F. Müller.

Laiou, A. E. (1981) The role of women in Byzantine society. *Jahrbuch der österreichischen Byzantinistik* 31, 233–260.

Laiou, A, E. (2009) Family structure and the transmission of property. In J. F. Haldon (ed.) *The Social History of Byzantium*, 51–75. Chichester, Wiley-Blackwell.

Lemerle, P. (1979–1989) *Les plus anciens recueils des miracles de saint Démétrius et la pénétration des Slaves dans les Balkans*. Paris, Éditions du Centre National de la Recherche Scientifique.

Manning, W. H. (1986) *Catalogue of the Romano-British Iron Tools, Fittings and Weapons in the British Museum*. London, British Museum.

Merton, R. K. (2007) On sociological theories of the middle range [1949]. In C. J. Calhoun (ed.) *Classical Sociological Theory*, 2nd ed., 448–459. Malden, Blackwell.

Milinković, M. (2007) Stadt oder 'Stadt': Frühbyzantinische Siedlungsstrukturen im nördlichen Illyricum. In J. Henning (ed.) *Post-Roman Towns, Trade and Settlement in Europe and Byzantium: Byzantium, Pliska and the Balkans*, 159–191. Millennium-Studien: Studien zu Kultur und Geschichte des ersten Jahrtausends n. Chr. 5(2). Berlin, de Gruyter.

Netting, R. M. (2002) *Smallholders, Householders: Farm Families and the Ecology of Intensive, Sustainable Agriculture*. 2nd ed. Stanford, Stanford University Press.

Papanikola-Bakirtzi, D. (2013) Household furnishings. In A. Drandaki, D. Papanikola-Bakirtzi, & A. G. Tourta (eds.) *Heaven and Earth*, 218–222. Athens, Hellenic Republic Ministry of Culture and Sports.

Rautman, M. L. (2006) *Daily Life in the Byzantine Empire*. Westport, Greenwood Press.

Russel, J. (2000) Household furnishings. In C. Kondoleon (ed.) *Antioch: The Lost Ancient City*, 79–89. Princeton, Princeton University Press.

Saradi, H. G. (2014) The city in Byzantine hagiography. In S. Efthymiadis (ed.) *The Ashgate Research Companion to Byzantine Hagiography: II Genres and Contexts*, 419–452. Farnham, Ashgate.

Sénécheau, M. (2014) Natürliche Arbeitsteilung zwischen Mann und Frau? Rollenbilder in Schulbüchern. In B. Röder (ed.) *Ich Mann. Du Frau: Feste Rollen seit Urzeiten?*, 70–83. Berlin, Rombach.

Smith, M. E. (2011) Empirical urban theory for archaeologists. *Journal of Archaeological Method and Theory* 18 (3), 167–192.

Sommer, U. (1990) Dirt theory, or archaeological sites seen as rubbish heaps. *Journal of Theoretical Archaeology* 1, 47–60.

Wachsmuth, K. (ed.) (1884) *Ioannis Stobaei anthologii libri duo priores, qui inscribi solent eclogae physicae et ethicae*. 2 vols. Berlin, Weidmann.

Whitby, M. & Whitby, M. (1997) *The History of Theophylact Simocatta: An English translation with introduction and notes*. Oxford, Oxford University Press.

Wilk, R. R. & Rathje, W. L. (1982) Household archaeology. *The American Behavioral Scientist* 26 (6), 617–639.

Chapter 7

Medieval churches in a borderland: The case of Transylvania

Daniela Marcu Istrate

Introduction

Medieval Transylvania was a borderland region between Byzantine Christianity, the steppe peoples and Latin Europe. Towards the end of the first millennium this region developed alternatively under the influence or the domination of several successive powers that managed to impose themselves: the Bulgarian Tsardom, the steppe empires and, the last one but the mightiest of them all, the Kingdom of Hungary, which, after its official Christianization in the Latin rite around the year 1000 became one of the most powerful states in Central Europe (Comşa 1960; Engel 2001, 1–7; Curta 2002, 272–277; Iambor 2005, 224–230). Hungary conquered Transylvania in several stages, from the 10th to the 13th century, advancing from the north to the south, by subjecting a number of political entities whose rulers were mentioned as *knezes* or *voievodes* (dukes) (Horedt 1986, 59–110; Heitel 1995, 415). At the time, the local Romanian-Slavic population belonged to the Greek-rite church, probably making use of several churches built mainly from wood and clay. No archaeological records concerning this issue have been discovered so far. As for the stone architecture, no church has been preserved intact, however some ruins may be attributed to the period. They were located in important settlements, mentioned as such in the contemporary written sources (Móré Heitel 2010, 11–20) (Fig. 7.1).

The integration of Transylvania in catholic Hungary set the development of this region on a new course. The royal administration enlisted some religious and military orders for organizing the territory, defending the borders, creating a religious network and ensuring the primacy of the Latin Church. Guests from Central Europe, mentioned in the written sources as *Teutonici, Fandrenses* and *Saxones,* were also invited to settle in the southern parts of the intra-Carpathian territories, being granted with important privileges, as known from a charter issued by King Andrew II in 1224 (Nägler 1992,

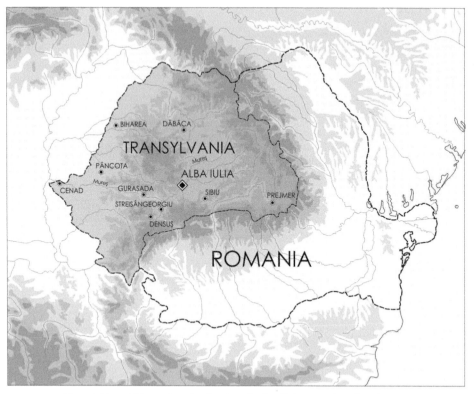

Fig. 7.1: Map of Transylvania showing the localities mentioned in the text

147–148). The most important area of colonization was southern Transylvania, where settlements were established around Alba Iulia and Sibiu in the 11th and 12th centuries. Then, in the 13th century, these colonies spread along the Carpathians. It was through these settlements that Romanesque architecture penetrated the region, leading to the construction of numerous basilicas (Crîngaci-Țiplic 2011, 66–87). Concurrently, the Szeklers, a population related to the Magyars, were placed in the eastern part of Transylvania (Benkő 2009, 13–17).

The coexistence of such different populations in a relatively restricted area led to a complicated ecclesiastical administration and produced a hybrid architectural landscape. The contacts between civilizations fostered the appearance of many fusion buildings, which appropriated ideas and shapes from multiple directions. On the other side, the ethnic diversity of the area engendered many unique structures and encouraged the development of a regional architecture, whose characteristics were dependent on the wealth, education and religion of the founders and owners. The medieval ecclesiastical landscape was dominated by Catholic churches erected under the influence of Romanesque and Gothic European art, the main types being the single-nave church and the basilica. The beginnings of this architecture date from the 11th century and by the year 1200 it had started to produce monuments of exceptional value. The most representative of these is St Michael's Cathedral in Alba Iulia (Entz 1958; Vătășianu 1959, 43–55; Sarkadi 2010).

The native population remained faithful to Oriental Christianity, being subordinated to certain structures operating in the neighbouring states. A specific architecture continued to develop mainly in the peripheral area of the province, under the influence of the Byzantine architecture but often using builders from Catholic construction sites. Some of the oldest medieval churches of Transylvania belong to the Orthodox architecture: the church in Streisângeorgiu has been dated archaeologically to the early 12th century, while those in Densuș and Gurasada may be even older (Popa 1988, 225–237, 265–272; Iambor 2005, 178–208).

As in other parts of Europe, medieval architecture is preserved fragmentarily and unevenly. Currently, more than 700 sites have churches or remnants of churches built before 1450, an outstanding heritage by all accounts. Even at a cursory exploration, this religious landscape expresses extreme diversity, mirroring the complex, multi-ethnic society that shaped it, including strong influences both from Latin Europe and from the Byzantine commonwealth. However, the surviving buildings show, at best, the realities of the 14th and 15th centuries, when most churches were modified or rebuilt in Gothic style, or turned into fortified spaces (Fabini 2009, 50–51). Consequently, very few of still standing churches preserve their original appearance from medieval times.

The early history of local religious architecture remained predominantly a topic of archaeological works, given that written sources are nearly non-existent. Though Transylvanian church archaeology is not very advanced, recent large-scale excavations have brought to light rich archaeological data and the ruins of some stone buildings dating back to the 10th and 11th century. This body of evidence has completely changed the image of the early ecclesiastical landscape and asks for a re-evaluation of the beginning of church history north of the Danube (Iambor 2005, 190–191, 273; Móré Heitel 2006, 54).

This paper concerns Alba Iulia, which was the major ecclesiastical site of medieval Transylvania. The history of its churches, as seen through recent excavations, illustrates not only the emergence of religious architecture, but also the Christianization process and the fluctuation of the local church between Byzantine and Latin Rule. The discussion is organised into five sections: the historical background of the site as a powerful central place, the Byzantine-style church, the first catholic cathedral and the second one and the conclusion.

Location and premises

Alba Iulia is located on the Mureș Valley, in the central-southern area of Transylvania. Its history has been clearly delineated since the Roman times, when it was known as *Apulum*. Its valuable strategic position and the proximity of important natural resources propelled it among the most important places of the Roman province Dacia. A *castrum* (Roman camp) was built for the *Legio XIII Gemina* and a large town developed nearby. After the abandonment of Dacia in the 3rd century, the *castrum* was inhabited by different populations and in the 9th century it became the headquarters

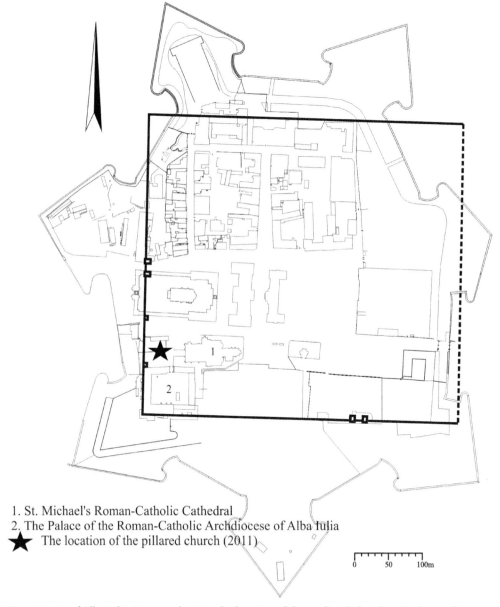

1. St. Michael's Roman-Catholic Cathedral
2. The Palace of the Roman-Catholic Archdiocese of Alba Iulia
★   The location of the pillared church (2011)

Fig. 7.2: Map of Alba Iulia Fortress, showing the location of the medieval churches, in the south-western corner of the Roman castrum

of a local political entity. Then, towards the end of the 11th century, the buildings of the See of the Diocese of Transylvania were erected in the southwestern corner of the ancient fortification which would be reorganised as a medieval fortress. This transformation was completed by the end of the 13th century and major changes did not occur thereafter until the 18th century, when the *castrum* was replaced with a Vauban fortification. Some parts of the Roman enclosure wall, gates and towers can still be seen in the modern town (Rusu 1979, 58; Anghel 1994, 286–287; Marcu Istrate 2009, 19–27) (Fig. 7.2).

In the centuries prior to the year 1000 the Roman fort provided a favourable setting for the emergence of a centre of power, which probably controlled the nearby salt mines and traffic alongside the Mureş River. Archaeological finds revealed an intense habitation not only in the *castrum* but also in its surroundings (Ciugudean, Pinter & Rustoiu 2006, 114–115; Ciugudean 2007, 248; Marcu Istrate 2009, 29–37). A settlement arose within the Roman walls, whose material culture belonged to the Byzantine commonwealth. Several cemeteries have been discovered in the proximity, used by Christian, pagan or mixed populations (Heitel 1975, 4–6; 1985, 225; Anghel 1994, 286–287).

Alba Iulia was conquered in the early 11th century and shortly thereafter the See of the Catholic Diocese of Transylvania was moved there. There are many unknowns in this period, however the elevation of Alba Iulia to the seat of a

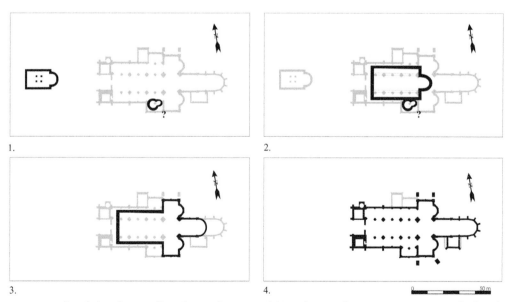

Fig. 7.3: Medieval churches in Alba Iulia: 1. The ruins of the 10th- to 11th-century Byzantine-style church and the restitution of the 9th- to 12th-century (?) round church (reconstructed plan, according to Heitel 1985, fig. 1) 2. The first cathedral, 11th and 12th centuries 3–4. Development of the ground plan of the second cathedral, 12th and 13th centuries; 16th- to 18th-century extensions in gray

Fig. 7.4: The apse of the round church, marked inside of St Michael's Cathedral

bishop shows a settlement of certain significance, with a longstanding tradition as a powerful central place (Engel 2001, 23–25, 44–45). The political and religious major changes were poorly reflected by contemporary written sources, but left behind an invaluable material legacy: the ecclesiastical architecture.

Currently, only one medieval church is still standing in Alba Iulia: St Michael's Roman Catholic Cathedral, erected during the 13th century in late Romanesque and early Gothic styles (Vătășianu 1959, 42–57) (Fig. 7.3). Nevertheless, extensive archaeological research conducted in the area of the cathedral has shown that three other religious buildings operated there before the year 1200: a Byzantine-style church with four central pillars, a round church and a basilica (Heitel 1985, 223–226; Marcu Istrate 2009, 77–84). Of these, the rotunda is a confusing monument, with an uncertain timeline: it could not be established if it is older than the basilica or if it was a baptistery attached to it (Heitel 1972, 151; Entz 1958, 6; Bóna 1990, 158) (Fig. 7.4). In contrast, it is certain that the pillared church functioned during the second part of the 10th and for most of the 11th century, to be replaced by a Romanesque basilica in the late 11th century (Figs 7.3 and 7.4).

The pillared church

The church was built in the southwestern corner of the *castrum*, an area which had been preferred for habitation and burial during previous centuries, probably because of its very good visibility over a fairly broad region along the Mureș Valley. The ruins were uncovered in 2011, in a bountiful archaeological context that allowed for an accurate chronological assignment (Marcu Istrate 2015, 180–186) (Figs 7.5 and 7.6).

The church, measuring about 21 × 12 m, consists of a rectangular nave and a semicircular apse with a 6.5 m wide opening towards the nave. In the centre of the nave there is a 4.5 × 4.5 m quadrangle enclosed by four pillars. The average thickness of the foundation was 1.3 m, with a maximum of 1.7 m at the northern corner of the nave. The foundations were built of river stone, limestone fragments and Roman bricks reused from the nearby Roman vestiges. This uneven material was set in the bedding trench carefully, so as to leave as few gaps as possible. Among the stones there are small amounts of clay and, randomly, of mortar, consisting primarily of white lime mixed with crushed brick. At the contemporary ground level, a thick layer of white crumbly mortar with small fragments of brick and lime pellets was applied over the foundation. The mortar layer underlays an upper structure of roughly hewn

Fig. 7.5: General view of the site: St. Michael's Roman-Catholic Cathedral and the ruins of the Byzantine-style church

stone blocks, probably alternated with courses of bricks, bound with thick layers of mortar. The interior ground level consisted of a mortar sheet that preserves traces of rectangular stone slabs and bricks (Figs 7.7 and 7.8).

A very coherent archaeological context and C14 analysis have shown that the church was built around mid-10th century and lasted for about a century. It ranks thus among the oldest religious buildings in the region, alongside those in Dăbâca, Cenad, Biharea and Pâncota (Iambor 2005, 178–208; Móré Heitel 2010, 21–38, 113–158).

What makes this church different from others is its central layout, a variant of the *Greek cross inscribed in a square*. The ground plan of the Greek cross inscribed in a square is the most characteristic planimetry of Byzantine ecclesiastical architecture. The emergence of this layout is linked with the period in which numerous oratories were built in the imperial palace of Constantinople. The so called *Nea Ekklesia*, a church founded by Emperor Basil I in 881, is usually seen by researchers at the origin of this layout. This very impressive building is known only from descriptions since it was destroyed in the late 15th century. Its architecture was increasingly imitated after the year 900, not only in Constantinople but also everywhere around the capital: in the major cities of the empire, in the bordering areas and in the neighbouring states. The shape and details fully matured at the beginning of the second millennium, enjoying subsequently a great popularity in the Byzantine world

Fig. 7.6: General view of the Byzantine-style church at the end of the archaeological investigation, September 2011

and all around it, up until the fall of Constantinople and beyond. The spread of this architectural style continued long after this date within the Balkan regions and in the Russian territories (Mango 1981, 194; Krautheimer 1986, 334–370; Bouras 2006, 48–163; Ćurčić 2010, 263–344).

Of the numerous churches of this kind that must have existed in 10th-century Constantinople, only two survived to some extent: Fenari Isa Camii and Bodrum Camii. They both have comparable proportions: Fenari Isa Camii has overall outer dimensions of 21 × 16 m, with a nave measuring 13 × 9.5 m, in which the columns define a quadrangle of 5 m on the sides; the nave of Bodrum Camii measures 10.5 × 8.8

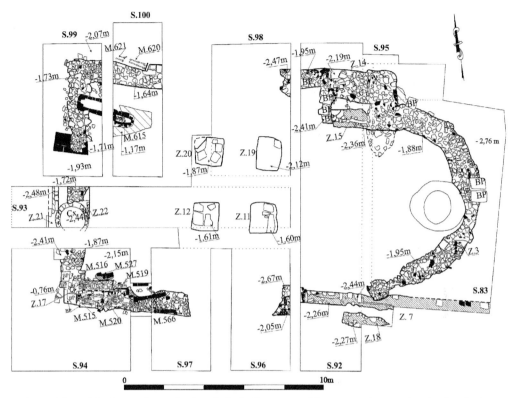

Fig. 7.7: *Plan of the Byzantine-style church, including some of the graves that cut into its foundations*

Fig. 7.8: *The apse and the northern wall of the church, as seen from the north-west*

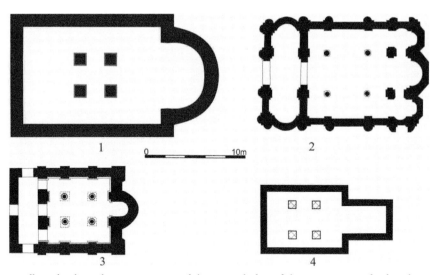

Fig. 7.9: 1. Alba Iulia, hypothetic restitution of the ground plan of the Byzantine-style church 2. Bodrum Camii (according to Krautheimer 1986, 356, fig. 309) 3. Pliska, one of the palace churches (according to Mijatev 1974, 103, fig. 109) 4. Modrá (according to Cibulka 1958, 27, fig. 17)

m and the pillared quadrangle is a square with 4.5 m sides (Krautheimer 1986, 356–361, figs 308–314). Similar examples can be found on the territory of the Bulgarian Tsardom, at a smaller scale. A chapel of the Palace of Pliska provides a suitable analogy: it has a single apse, a square nave of 6.3 × 6.5 m, with a central space dominated by four pillars and a narrow narthex (Mijatev 1974, 102–103, fig. 109) (Fig. 7.9).

If the archaeologically uncovered church in Alba Iulia is to be considered in this general historical and architectural context, it is obvious that it was similar in size to the churches in Constantinople; however, it was substantially larger than the Bulgarian contemporary examples. In relation to the classical ground plan, the Alba Iulia church presents the peculiarity of a single large apse, compared to which the bay of the pillars is narrower, so it can be defined as a *provincial variant* of the Greek cross inscribed in a square layout. The current fragmentary state of knowledge in the field of medieval Byzantine architecture certainly explains why this variant has not been identified so far. It could not have a singular occurrence in Alba Iulia, a site in which there was, in fact, no tradition or experience regarding buildings made of stone. The last such constructions had been erected there in Roman times, perhaps with the sole exception of the above-mentioned rotunda.

The pillared church must have belonged to a series of medieval buildings that originally adapted the Byzantine prototype within the limits of what was practically achievable. There are no other similar edifices from the 10th or the 11th century – at least none that are known currently. Nevertheless, it is striking that a nearly identical building has been preserved in Transylvania, that is the church in Densuș, whose chronological frame is undecided (Vătășianu 1959, 89–95; Popa 1988, 228–230).

From an architectural point of view, this type displays the characteristics of a period in which the religious architecture crystallized in eastern Central Europe: the span between the 9th and the 13th century. A number of other unique ensembles are reported in the scientific literature. Examples of such cases are, for instance, the basilica in Fenékpuszta, on the Pannonian Plain (Curta 2005, 183), the rotunda in Preslav (Mango 1981, 173; Krautheimer 1986, 318–321) and the churches in Modra, in Moravia (Cibulka 1958) or Zselicszentjakab in Kaposvár, Hungary (Nagy 1973; Móré Heitel 2006, 41–42, 69–70). Such unique structures are also found on the territory of Transylvania: the Orthodox churches in Streisângeorgiu, Densuş and Gurasada, or the formerly Roman Catholic cross-shaped church in Prejmer (Marcu Istrate 2013). However, it is quite likely that 'uniqueness' in this field is a matter defined by the progress of the investigations, as the discovery in Alba Iulia has just shown.

In the present state-of-art, the pillared church is a unique occurrence in the area and, in fact, across the Carpathian Basin. Furthermore, it has a monumental appearance, comparable in size with churches from the capital of the Byzantine Empire. Architectural aspects apart, it is very important to clarify under what circumstances such a church could have been built north of the Danube, since the region was nigh inexistent from a Byzantine point of view. At that time, Transylvania was not part of the Byzantine territories proper, nor did it belong to the territories over which the Bulgarian Tsardom exercised effective suzerainty.

As an expression of an organised religious structure, such a church could have arisen only under the gaze of a powerful elite, whose authority had grown mid-10th century, very likely taking advantage of the diminishing Bulgarian influence in the area after the death of Tsar Simeon in 927 (Madgearu 2003). The choice of this type of architecture and even the construction technique indicates a founder faithful to the Byzantine church, even though the available data is insufficient for identifying it more precisely from an ethnic point of view. Whether it was a native elite that managed to maintain its position in the region, or a Hungarian elite, the emergence and service of this church cannot be detached from the Byzantine period of the religious history of Hungary, which left many other vestiges in Transylvania and beyond. This stage began with an event that took place in the middle of the 10th century and has been recounted in several written sources: Boulsoudes and Gyula, two Hungarian princes, were baptized at Constantinople, and Gyula brought home a Christianization mission led by Bishop Hierotheos (Moravcsik 1970, 108; Oikonomidès 1971, 532; Font 2005, 285–287).

Gyula's homeland was mentioned as *Tourkia*, but it is not known exactly whether this homeland was in Transylvania, with headquarters in Alba Iulia, or west of the Tisza. The arguments for the former include the Hungarian name of Alba Iulia – *Gyulafehérvár*, meaning Gyula`s white citadel, which resulted from the translation of the old Slavic name *Bălgrad* (the white citadel) added to the anthroponym *Gyula*. In support of the latter variant there are mentioned 10th century Byzantine artefacts discovered in the eastern part of present-day Hungary (Madgearu 2008). No matter where its centre of operations was – assuming it even had a certain headquarters – the Byzantine Christianization mission had considerable consequences and brought about an Orthodox hierarchy that survived in the Kingdom of Hungary in the form of a Metropolitan See until the 12th century (Oikonomidès 1971, 527-533; Baán 1999, 45–48). The progress of this mission must have included the building of churches: the only edifice that corresponds, both chronologically and architecturally, with this historical event is the pillared church in Alba Iulia. Its significant dimensions show that it was prepared for a large community, probably consisting of both local Christians and newcomers whose Christianization was underway. It is impossible to ascertain and, in fact, it is of little importance whether the one who consecrated the church was Bishop Hierotheos, an unknown member of his mission or his direct successor at the head of the Church of Tourkia.

The first cathedral

The political situation in the region and the relentless efforts of the papacy heavily tilted the balance between the Greek Church and the Latin Church in favour of the latter. A new, Latin mission of Christianization became active in the last decades of the 10th century. It gained ground and Hungarian Prince Vaik, baptized in the year 1000, became King Stephen and Hungary became a country of Western orientation. During the following centuries however, the country's broad religious tolerance allowed the Byzantine influence to manifest itself in various forms, including by maintaining some Orthodox churches and monasteries.

In 1002 King Stephen conquered Alba Iulia and thus occupied the vast territory that belonged to this centre of power. The documents recorded this event as the King's victory against a prince who had refused to become Christian and whose name was also Gyula, the same as the name of the prince baptized in the 10th century (Kristó 2004, 105–108). In fact, it is likely that 11th-century Gyula was a local prince faithful to the Greek church, the heir of the political-religious situation created earlier through the efforts of the 10th-century Gyula and those of Bishop Hierotheos. Defeating Gyula and conquering his headquarters had to be seen as decisive steps for strengthening the Hungarian rule in the Eastern Carpathian Basin. The most obvious consequence of this victory was the change of the ecclesiastical structure, transferring the See of the Diocese of Transylvania from the northern part of the province to Alba Iulia. The event maybe took place in the year 1009, but its concrete effects became visible only in late 11th century, when a cathedral appeared there. The first bishop was mentioned even later, in the early 12th century.

The first cathedral was built approximately 30 m east of the pillared church. Its ruins were discovered inside the present-day cathedral at the beginning of the 20th century. They were examined again in 1968–1977, but all that remains of these investigations is an outline plan and a few general data (Vătășianu 1959, 22–23; Heitel 1985, 216, 227–228). It appears to have been a three-aisled basilica, the central nave ending in an elongated, semicircular, almost horseshoe-shaped apse to the east. The aisles, separated by pillars, are assumed to have been vaulted. A slight thickening of the western wall suggests two towers on the main façade. The cathedral was certainly a much more imposing and attractive building than the old church: it was nearly twice as large, its silhouette was probably more slender and the decoration consisted of exceptional sculptural pieces, as suggested by the few preserved fragments.

The planning of the new construction was made in relation to the previous one, maintaining the same axis: it is clear that the pillared church was visible at the time, for otherwise the two could not have been positioned as if they were part of the same project. The new catholic church was erected nearby the Byzantine church but not in a direct connection to it: it was an attempt to consecrate an existing place of worship and to take advantage of its long-standing tradition and its worshipers. It is difficult to ascertain how things unfolded; however, making such an arrangement was also a way of changing the religious orientation of this major settlement from Constantinople to Rome. The attempt managed to do so, because Orthodoxy would make an official return in the area only many centuries later (Fig. 7.3).

The cathedral was built in the second half of the 11th century, possibly completed around 1100, as suggested by the archaeological evidence and some sculptural pieces recovered during restorations or reused for the present-day cathedral (Horedt 1986, 136–138; Bóna 1990, 159). Two very important events occurred in the same period: the demolition of the old church and the establishment of a burial ground (Fig. 7.10).

Fig. 7.10: Graves cut into the foundation of the south-western corner of the pillared church

The cemetery occupied a large area around the cathedral and almost abutted the former Roman enclosure in the west, including the area of the old church. The rich funerary inventory allowed assigning the beginnings of the graveyard to the last decades of the 11th century. Many graves cut into the ruins of the old church, destroying them almost entirely. This demonstrates once more that a major religious change had taken place in Alba Iulia during the late 11th century, and in the new structure the Byzantine-style church no longer had a place: it was demolished and its remains had no significance for the community that used the cemetery (Marcu Istrate 2015, 194).

The second cathedral

The first cathedral did not have a very long life: at the end of the 12th century, a new church started to be erected around it, reaching its final shape in the last decades of the 13th century (Figs 7.3 and 7.5). The building site experienced a number of stages, which can be perceived easily in the eclectic style of the church. St Michel's Cathedral is a Romanesque basilica with three aisles, a transept and a Gothic choir with a polygonal apse. The transept ends to the east in semicircular apses and to the west in rectangular chapels. In the beginning, the sanctuary also ended in a semicircular apse – the present-day Gothic choir was built during a later construction stage. The western façade was planned with two towers that were to bracket the main entrance, but only the southern one was completed.

The final result of this long construction site was truly exceptional: a building that is unique in the central-eastern area of Europe, both because of its ground plan and because of its decoration. The second cathedral has been preserved as such for centuries remaining almost intact with only a few additions and some minor changes that did not alter its medieval fabric. It is today the main architectural jewel of the citadel in Alba Iulia and an outstanding occurrence in the local religious landscape (Fig. 7.11).

Fig. 7.11: St Michael's Roman Catholic Cathedral, preserving the remains of the round church and of the first cathedral

Conclusion

The construction of an ecclesiastical structure dependent on Rome was a priority in 11th-century Transylvania.

The Latin Church replaced the older Greek Church and this affected not only the practised faith but also the ecclesiastical architecture. The archaeological investigations undertaken in some important religious sites argue for this change, which may have been symptomatic for the whole area.

Organising the Hungarian Latin Church, King Stephen established ten dioceses in early 11th century, one of them being the Diocese of Transylvania. It is presumed that the latter had for a long period itinerant headquarters, reflecting the progress of the conquest in the Carpathian Basin. Research on the diocesan history and possessions has resulted in locating the early phase of this institution in the northern half of Transylvania.

The See of the diocese moved to Bălgrad - later called Alba Iulia - in the second half of the 11th century and has remained there until today. It was the main consequence of the Hungarian conquest of the central-southern territory, more precisely of the Mureş River basin, by destroying a great secular power, whose Christianization had been shaped by a Byzantine mission. The most important result of its relationship with Byzantium was a *greek cross inscribed in a square church*, operating from mid-10th century to mid or late 11th century. The ruins of this church, uncovered archeologically in 2011, represent an important landmark not only in researching the history of Transylvania and Hungary, but also in the study of the Byzantine architecture.

Following the Hungarian conquest, the Byzantine-style church was replaced with a cathedral. The latter one is not very well known, however judging by its successor – the present-day cathedral – it must have been a monumental Romanesque building, created by stonemasons from western Central Europe. Taking into account the chronological clues offered by its cemetery, it may be assumed that it was built in the second half of the 11th century and lasted for roughly one century. During the 13th century, it was replaced with a larger, Romanesque-Gothic building, which has survived to our days as one of the most important religious monuments in the eastern Central Europe.

Bibliography

Anghel, G. (1994) Despre evoluția orașului antic, medieval și modern Alba Iulia. *Apulum* XXXI, 283–302.

Baán, I. (1999) The Metropolitanate of Tourkia. The organization of the Byzantine Church in Hungary in the Middle Ages. In G. Prinzing and M. Salamon (eds.) *Byzanz und Ostmitteleuropa 950-1453. Beiträgezueiner table-ronde des XIX International Congress of Byzantine Studies, Copenhagen 1996*, 45–55. Wiesbaden, Harrassowitz.

Benkő, E. (2009) Mittelalterliche archäologische Funde im Szeklerland. In H. Roht (ed.) *Die Szekler in Siebenbürgen. Von der privilegierten Sondergemeinschaft zur ethnischen Gruppe*, 13–43. Siebenbürgische Archiv 40. Koln-Weimar-Wien, Böhlau.

Bóna, I. (1990) Siebenbürgen im mittelalterlichen Königreich Ungarn. Zeit des ungarish-slawischen Zussamenlebens (895–1172). In B. Köpeczi (ed.) *Kurze Geschichte Siebenbürgen*, 107–172. Budapest, Akadémiai Kiadó.

Bouras, C. (2006) *Byzantine & Post-Byzantine Architecture in Greece*. Athens, Melissa Publishing House.

Cibulka, J. (1958) *Velkomoravský kostel v Modré u velehradu. a začátkz křesťanství na Moravě.* Praga, Nakladatelstvi Československé Akademie Véd.

Ciugudean, H. (2007) Pottery offerings in the early middle age cemetery of Alba Iulia „Staţia de Salvare". In C. Cosma (ed.) *Funerary offerings and votive depositions in Europe's 1st millennium AD. Cultural artefacts and local identities,* 243–257. Cluj-Napoca, Mega.

Ciugudean, H., Pinter, Z. K. & Rustoiu G. (2006) *Habitat, religie etnicitate. Descoperiri arheologice din sec. IX-XI în Transilvania.* Catalog de expoziţie. Alba Iulia, Altip.

Comşa, M. (1960) Die bulgarische Herrschaft nördlich der Donau während des IX. und X. Jhs. im Lichte der archäologische Forschungen. *Dacia New Series* IV, 395–422.

Crîngaci-Ţiplic, M. E. (2011) 'Oaspeţii germani' în sudul Transilvaniei. Istorie, arheologie şi arhitectură (secolele XII-XIII).* Bucureşti, Editura Academiei Române.

Ćurčić, S. (2010) *Architecture in the Balkans. From Diocletian to Süleyman the Magnificent.* New Haven and London, Yale University Press.

Curta, F. (2002) Transilvania în jurul anului 1000. *Ephemeris Napocensis* XII, 267–288.

Curta, F. (2005) Before Cyril and Methodius: Christianity and Barbarians beyond the sixth- and seventh-century Danube frontier. In F. Curta (ed.) *East Central and Eastern Europe in the Early Middle Ages,* 181-219. Ann Arbor, The University of Michigan Press.

Engel, P. (2001) *The Realm of St. Stephen. A History of Medieval Hungary, 895-1526.* London-New York, I. B. Tauris & Co Ltd.

Entz, G. (1958) La cathédrale de Gyulafehérvár (Alba Iulia). *Acta Historiae Artium* 5/1-2, 1–40.

Fabini, H. (2009) *Die Kirchenbürgen der Siebenbürger Sachsen.* Hermannstadt, Monumenta.

Font, M. (2005) Missions, conversions and power legitimization in east central Europe at the turn of the first Millenium. In F. Curta (ed.) *East Central and Eastern Europe in the Early Middle Ages,* 283–295. Ann Arbor, The University of Michigan Press.

Heitel, R. R. (1972) Archäologische Beiträge zu den romanischen Baudenkmälern aus Südsiebenbürgen. *Revue Roumaine d'Histoire de l'Art* 9/2, 39–160.

Heitel, R. R. (1975) Archäologische Beiträge zu den romanischen Baudenkmälern aus Südsiebenbürgen. II (in Zusammenhang mit der zeitlichen Bestimmung der ältesten 'Rotunda Ecclesia' Rumäniens und der Kathedrale I in Alba Iulia). *Revue Roumaine d'Histoire de l'Art* 12/1, 3–10.

Heitel, R. R. (1985) Principalele rezultate ale cercetărilor arheologice din zona sud-vestică a cetăţii de la Alba Iulia (1968–1977). I. *Studii şi cercetări de istorie veche şi arheologie* 36/3, 215–231.

Heitel, R. R. (1995) Die Archäologie der ersten und zweiten Phase des Eindringens der Ungarn in das innerkarpatische Transilvanien. *Dacia New Series* XXXVIII–XXXIX, 389–439.

Horedt, K. (1986) *Siebenbürgen im Frühmittelalter.* Bonn, Dr. Rudolf Habelt.

Iambor, P. (2005) *Aşezări fortificate din Transilvania (sec. IX-XIII).* Cluj-Napoca, Argonaut.

Krautheimer, R. (1986) *Early Christian and Byzantine architecture,* fourth edition. New Haven and London, Yale University Press.

Kristó, G. (2004) *Ardealul timpuriu (895-1324).* Biblioteca de Istorie Medievală din Szeged 20. Szeged, Szegedi Középkorász Mühely.

Madgearu, A. (2003) Transylvania and the Bulgarian Expansion in the 9th and 10th centuries. *Acta Musei Napocensis* 39-40/II, 41–62.

Madgearu, A. (2008) The mission of Hierotheos: locations and significance. *Byzantinoslavica* 6/1-2, 119–138.

Mango, C. (ed.) (1981) *Architecture Byzantine.* Paris, Berger Levrault.

Marcu Istrate, D. (2009) *Catedrala romano-catolică Sfântul Mihail şi palatul episcopal din Alba Iulia. Cercetări arheologice 2000-2002.* Alba Iulia, Altip.

Marcu Istrate, D. (2013) Neue Erkenntnisse zu den Anfängen der Tartlauer Kirche. In K. Gündisch (ed.) *General probe Burzenland. Neue Forschungen zur Geschichte des Deutschen Ordens in Siebenbürgen und im Banat,* 132–153. Siebenbürgische Archiv 42. Köln-Weimar-Wien, Böhlau.

Marcu Istrate, D. (2015) Byzantine influences in the Carpathian Basin around the turn of the Millennium. The pillared church of Alba Iulia. *Dacia New Series* LIX, 177–213.

Mijatev, K. (1974) *Die mittelalterliche Baukunst in Bulgarien.* Sofia, Verlag der Bulgarischen Akademie der Wissenschaften.

Moravcsik, G. (1970) *Byzantium and the Magyars.* Budapest, Akadémiai Kiadó.

Móré Heitel, S. (2006) *Abația de la Pâncota și vestigiile ei.* Cluj-Napoca, Mega.

Móré Heitel, S. (2010) *Începuturile artei medievale în bazinul inferior al Mureșului.* Timișoara, Excelsior Art.

Nägler, Th. (1992) *Die Ansiedlung der Siebenbürgen Sachsen.* Bukarest, Kriterion.

Nagy, E. (1973) Elözetes jelentés a kaposszentjakabi apátság feltárásáról. *Somogyi Múzeumok Közleményei* 1, 335–339.

Oikonomidès, N. (1971) Á propos des relations ecclésiastiques entre Byzance et la Hongrie au Xe siècle: le métropolite de Turquie. *Revue des Études Sud-est Européennes* 9, 527–533.

Popa, R. (1988) *La începuturile evului mediu românesc. Țara Hațegului.* București, Editura Științifică și Enciclopedică.

Rusu, M. (1979) Castrul roman Apulum și cetatea feudală de la Alba Iulia. *Anuarul Institutului de Istorie și Arheologie Cluj-Napoca* XXII, 47–70.

Sarkadi, M. (2010) „s folytatva magát a régi művet" Tanulmányok a gyulafehérvári székesegyház és püspöki palota történetéről. Budapest, Teleki László Alapítvány.

Vătășianu, V. (1959) *Istoria artei feudale în Țările Române*, I. București, Editura Academiei Române.

Chapter 8

Petrapilosa: The architectural and historical development of the structure

Josip Višnjić

Introduction

There are a number of reasons why medieval feudal fortifications constitute first rate archaeological sites in terms of the opportunities to collect data on the life and functioning of a very specific aspect of medieval society. Petrapilosa, built in the north of the Istrian peninsula in present day Croatia, is an excellent example of such a site. This is an area in which the Adriatic Sea reaches deepest into the European mainland and where the mixing of Mediterranean and Central European influences created specific political relationships in the Middle Ages. It was fertile ground for the conflicts that marked the period of the Istrian high and late medieval and early post-medieval periods. Given the robust development of feudal relationships and frequent conflicts, the large number of feudal fortifications in the rural Istrian landscape is not surprising (Fig. 8.1).

Petrapilosa was in use in the period from the 11th to 17th century and is, in this context, of great interest due to its developed archaeological stratigraphy and the eminently distinguishable development of its architecture. It functioned actively throughout the entire period in which feudal fortifications were the major hubs of the Istrian peninsula, making it a prime example of the development of these fortifications and a paragon for their interpretation in this area. Furthermore, the fact that sites in Istria dating to the high and late medieval periods were not of archaeological interest until about a decade ago, again underscores the importance of this site.

Archaeological research of the site is part of a project that aims to effect the rehabilitation and conservation of the preserved architectural remains of the fortification, conducted under the leadership of the Croatian Ministry of Culture and the Croatian Conservation Institute. A significant part of the site has been researched over the past six years and a great quantity of data has been collected that sheds light

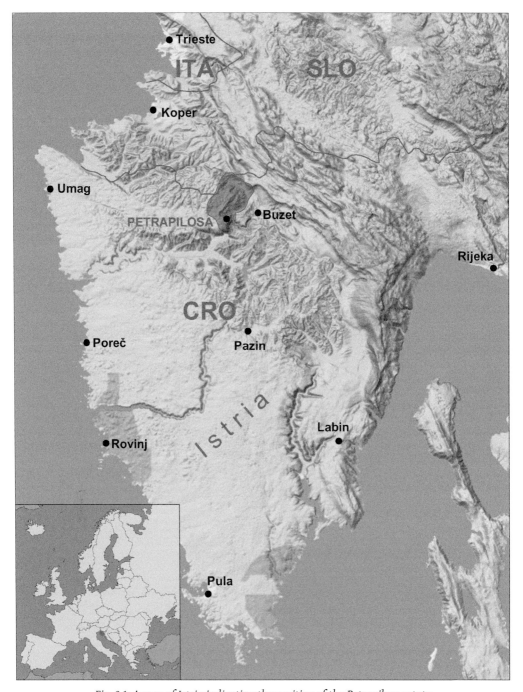

Fig. 8.1: A map of Istria indicating the position of the Petrapilosa estate

on the development of the fortification and positions it in the historical context to which it belongs.

Description of the architectural survey

Petrapilosa is situated at a strategically excellent position, rising high above the surrounding terrain (Fig. 8.2). It is surrounded on three sides by steep slopes and cliffs and is accessible only from the west. The fortress' elongated floor plan, running from east to west, makes use of all the available space (Fig. 8.3). The complex consists of two core sections: the central and outer body of the fortification. It is clearly evident in the walls of the fortress that it developed and was expanded over time, with the central core forming the nucleus from which the fortress developed. In its final phase of development it consisted of a central tower, palace and inner courtyard with several auxiliary buildings. The entrance to the central part of the complex was located on its eastern wall. Past the gate one enters a narrow, L-shaped corridor,

Fig. 8.2: Aerial view of Petrapilosa from the south

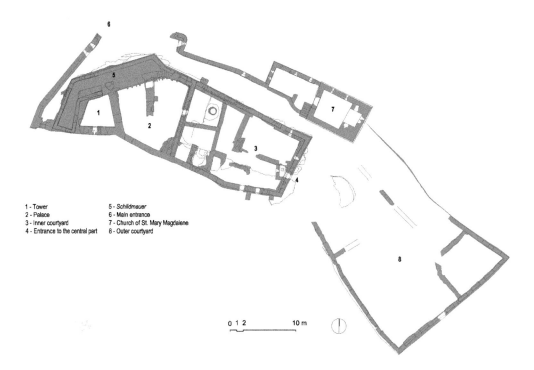

1 - Tower					5 - *Schildmauer*
2 - Palace					6 - Main entrance
3 - Inner courtyard				7 - Church of St. Mary Magdalene
4 - Entrance to the central part		8 - Outer courtyard

0 1 2					10 m

Fig. 8.3: Ground plan of the fortification

navigated by stairs hewn into the living rock. The corridor was controlled by an arrowslit in the wall opposite the entrance and an opening in the barrel-vaulted ceiling. The corridor opened to the inner courtyard, occupying the eastern half of the central section of the fortification. Auxiliary buildings, now recognisable by the remains of their foundations, occupied the courtyard. The tower was situated at the point most exposed to attack and constituted the strongpoint of the defence, with walls up to 4 m thick. The palace of the fortification was adjoined to the tower and had four storeys.

The outer section of the fortification was situated between the central and outer ramparts. It encompassed the central area to all sides but the south, where this was not possible, but also not necessary, given the cliff located here. The gate to the complex was located on the western wall and was controlled by the central tower (Fig. 8.4). The small church of St Mary Magdalene was situated in the outer section with a bell gable at the façade and a rectangular, barrel vaulted apse (Fig. 8.5). This small church shows characteristics of Romanesque sacral architecture (Marušić 1974, 22; Šonje 1982, 131). Traces of the frescoes that once adorned the interior of the church, which can be dated to the 15th century (Krnjak 2003, 14), were found during archaeological excavations conducted in 1995 by the Archaeological museum of Istria from Pula. A courtyard opens to the east of the church and the central section, also

Fig. 8.4: Aerial view of Petrapilosa from the north

Fig. 8.5: The Church of St Mary Magdalene

occupied by various auxiliary buildings and enclosed by relatively well-preserved walls on the crowns of which the remains of crenellations can be identified. An interesting specimen of a medieval toilet is situated in the narrow space between the western wall of the tower and the outer ramparts. This is a small room, once covered by a mono-pitched roof, with a small narrow window and a stone slab with a square opening above the cliff.

The exceptionally poor condition of the preserved architecture of the fortification, some walls of which were truly on the brink of a collapse that would have threatened to permanently degrade this cultural monument, had for some time prompted initiatives to launch a remediation project. A systematic remediation project at Petrapilosa was finally launched in 2009 which encompassed the production of quality architectural and photogrammetric survey using the 3D scanning method, systematic archaeological excavations and remediation work on preserved architectural remains.

Historical data on Petrapilosa

A full appreciation of the extent of the layered complexity of this site requires at least a cursory consideration of the data provided to us about Petrapilosa by historical written sources. The earliest historical data that individual early authors associated with this fortification are from the second half of the 10th century. In 965, namely, the patriarch Rodoald granted to the bishop of Poreč the Ruin fortification that had been 'demolished by the Slavs and barbarians' (Corbanese 1984, 320; Darovec 1996, 16; Sirk 2002, 177). The basis of the assumption was the link that De Franceschi postulated between the toponyms Petrapilosa and Ruin. He postulated that German medieval written sources altered the name into *Ruenstein,* the name that appears in a document from the year 1275 (Bianchi 1847, 205), which was literally translated in Latin sources as *Petra Pilosa,* and later into the Italian form *Pietrapelosa* (De Franceschi 1852, 51). Although he subsequently abandoned the idea, the majority of authors nevertheless accepted this interpretation (Benussi 1897, 101–102; Klen 1976, 30; Kirac 1990; Darovec 1996, 17). Besides in the cited document from 965, derivatives of this name can be found in documents dated to the 11th and 12th centuries. The *Ruvin* fortification is again mentioned in the early 11th century, which Duke Henry, later Emperor Henry II, granted to the church in Aquileia (Bianchi 1847, 224; De Franceschi 1852, 51; Benussi 1897, 291; Benedetti 1964, 7; Klen 1976, 29; Darovec 1996, 17). A hundred years later, in 1102, the Istrian Count Ulrik II and his wife Adelaide awarded the church in Aquileia significant territory in Istria, including the village of *Druvine* (CDI 1 1986, 241–242; Kandler 1875, 241; Klen 1976, 30; Darovec 1996, 17). The archaeological research conducted thus far has not demonstrated the functioning of the fortification in this early phase, further bringing this hypothesis into question.

It is in the 13th century that historical sources begin explicitly mentioning a fortification bearing the name Petrapilosa and owners that associate their name to that of the fortification. The emergence of the Petrapilosa family corresponds with the moment at which the Aquileian patriarchs become Istrian margraves, and the Petrapilosa's were evidently their vassals ruling this holding. The first well-known feudal landholder from this powerful aristocratic family was *Vulginius de Petrapilosa*, mentioned in a document from the year 1210 (Kos 1928, no. 166; Benedetti 1964, 7; Darovec 1996, 19; Sirk 2002, 177). This family administered the fortification over the coming century and a half while ruling the lands to the north and south of the upper course of the Mirna River, Petrapilosa and Grožnjan, wielding a strong influence in the administration of Motovun and are numbered among the leading Istrian aristocratic families of the period (Darovec 1996, 26). After Vulginius sources mention Vikard Petrapilosa as a witness to the signing of various agreements (Darovec 2007, 51–53), then the brothers Carsteman and Henry who were, among other matters, caught up in the conflicts that gripped the Istrian peninsula in the second half of the 13th century, in which they lost their lives (CDI 2 1986, 289–604; Darovec 2007, 53–67). The most frequently mentioned member of the family is Vikard II Petrapilosa. This is a result of the long period over which his activities can be followed (1287–1330), but also his proclivity for the conflicts occurring across Istria and Friuli (CDI 2 1986, 757-770; CDI 2 1986, 838; Darovec 2007, 71–77). His successor, Peter, also embroiled in various conflicts in Istria, found himself in financial straits. His efforts to resolve this issue included a round of, ultimately unfruitful, negotiations with the Venetians in 1335 on the sale of the fortification (Minotto 1887, 19.3.1335; Darovec 2007, 79–83). The last representative of the Petrapilosa's, Nicholas, is mentioned in a 1352 document (CDI 3 1986, 1253) after which a mention of this once powerful Istrian aristocratic family cannot be found.

The next owner of the fortification was Volrik Rihemberg, who in 1355 once again undertook to sell Petrapilosa to the Venetians. This effort again proved fruitless on account of unresolved legal relations (Minotto 1888, 3.12.1355). The fortification remained under the ownership of the patriarchate up to the year 1421 when it, along with Oprtalj and Buzet – its last holdings in Istria, wound up in Venetian hands. The final decades of the patriarchate's presence on the peninsula saw marquises holding Petrapilosa as its representatives in the province (CDI 3 1986, 1335; 1363; Minotto 1887, 272; 1888, 288–289; Darovec 2007, 109–117).

Following the Venetian conquest, the fortification was assigned in 1440 to Nicolo Gravisi, an aristocrat based in Kopar-Piran. From that point through to 1869, when feudal obligations were finally abolished in the Monarchy, the Gravisi family remained owners of this estate (Darovec 1996, 48; Flego 2000). The fortification itself was ravaged by fire in the 1620s and was most likely not subsequently reconstructed (Klen 1976, 22). There are documents that confirm that there was an initiative among the members of the Gravisi family to rebuild the fortress (Senato Mare 1899, 71), but the idea, it appears, was never seen through. The last edifice to remain in use was the small church of St Mary Magdalene, at which the last mass was celebrated in 1793 (Darovec 1996, 51), indicating that the fortification may have been used on a limited scale up to that date.

The results of the archaeological research to date

Archaeological research was another prerequisite to the unhampered conduct of remediation work on the architectural remains of the fortification. It was necessary as a means of gathering all unknown but necessary data subsequently used when adopting decisions on the most adequate methods of conserving and presenting individual segments of the architectural complex, as the most adequate method of gathering data on the multi-century use of this fortress and as a method of gathering original construction material for the reconstruction of historical structures.

For the cited reasons, in campaigns to date, archaeological research preceded all construction work, and the fortification's palace area and a part of its inner and outer courtyard has been researched. Archaeological research has uncovered some previously unknown details concerning the development of the fortress and its functioning. Given the nature of the paper and the limited space, all of the finds shall not be described in greater detail, rather only a summary overview shall be provided. Individual functional sections of the fortification have been discovered in the course of the research to date, such as various remains of the foundations of structures from different phases of its development, cisterns situated along the eastern wall of the palace, which belongs to one of the early phases of the fortification's development or, for example, architectural remains that establish the gradual expansion of the outer courtyard area (Višnjić, 2012a). But perhaps the most valuable information it has yielded is a rich stratigraphy sequence that covers an unbroken period of the fortress' use from the 11th to 17th century. This is particularly significant in light of the fact that the high medieval period has been very poorly archaeologically researched in Istria and that it is in fact multilayered archaeological sites that are key to all future archaeological research of sites of similar characteristics.

The most representative example of the stratigraphy can be found in the area of the northern section of the palace, and it will serve as model for its presentation (Fig. 8.6). The oldest layers yielded a small number of ceramic finds that confirm the use of this site in prehistory, i.e. the Bronze Age, while all other layers are attributable to medieval and early post-medieval utilisation.

The data acquired from the research to date indicates that the medieval fortification was most likely erected in the 11th century. When dating this group of finds, i.e. the corresponding stratigraphic unit, it should be noted that samples of charcoal have been extracted from it in the area of the palace and inner courtyard in the course of the research conducted to date and submitted for radiocarbon analysis. The analyses have shown that the corresponding layer can most likely be dated to the 11th century. The charcoal sample from the palace (an analysis of the samples under laboratory number LTL 5778A was conducted at the CEDAD, AMS and radiocarbon facility of the University of Lecce in Italy), namely, yielded an absolute dating of from AD 1030–1170 (68.2%), or AD 1020–1220 (95.4%), while the sample taken from the inner courtyard (an analysis of the samples under laboratory number PP13SJ1083U6 was conducted at

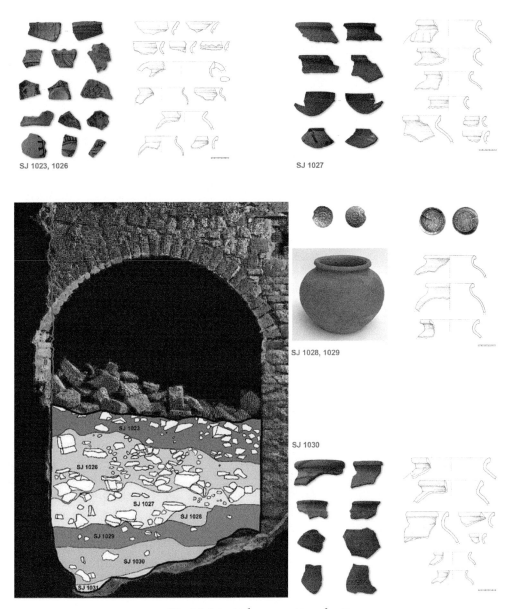

Fig. 8.6: A typical cross-section of a site

the Beta Analytic Inc. in Miami, USA) yielded an absolute dating of from AD 1040–1160 (68%), or AD 1025–1190 (95%), such that these data can serve as points of reference in the interpretation of the creation of this fortification, which is of great importance given the complete lack of comparative material in Istria.

A large quantity of potsherds was found in the oldest medieval layer, SU 1030, that show certain specificity in comparison with other layers (Fig. 8.6: SJ 1030; Fig. 8.7: 1, 2). Basically, these are sherds of globular pots that can be grouped based on the shape of their rims and for which a relatively good dating parallels can be found in Istria (Marušić 1971, T. XXXVII: 1, 2; T. XXXVIII: 1; T. XXXIX: 1; Terrier *et al.* 2007, 215, T. B1, B2, A1, A3) and in the neighboring Hrvatsko primorje region (northern Croatian littoral) and Slovenia (Stadler 1995, cat. A77–A84; Cetinić 1999, 87; Jarnej 2001, 465, T1: 1–3; Predovnik 2003, 58, cat. 1–22; Bekić 2006, 219, T13: 1–5).

The following group of finds include sherds gathered in layers SU 1029, 1038 and the burnt layer SU 1037 (Fig. 8.6: SJ 1028, 1029; Fig. 8.7: 5–8). Parallels to the most numerous group of finds among the currently published material from the Istrian peninsula can not be found, and this may be due to insufficient research, but it may, alternatively, indicate the influx of cultural influences coming to Petrapilosa at the time from other directions. The best parallels to this vessel form can be found in northern Italy (Rigoni 1992, T. 2: 12; Beltrame & Colussa 2002, T. 2: 18, 20, 21; Piuzzi *et al.* 2003, 104, 4; Villa 2004, fig. 14: 1, 2, 4; Negri 2007, note 33; T. 2: 15; Ferri *et al.* 2008, T. 2: 1, 6) where they are dated to the period from the 11th to 13th century. Given the cited parallels, a dating reliable coin find that will be described in detail further in the text and the fact that this period terminated in an event that was, judging by the burnt layer SU 1037, destructive in nature, and that can very likely be identified with the historically confirmed attacks against the fortification in the second half of the 13th century, this period can be dated to the 12th and 13th centuries.

Two coin finds were made in the course of the research related to the layers in question. Although perhaps not particularly impressive at first glance, these finds do significantly facilitate our understanding of the stratigraphic relationships of the layers at the site, and thereby also facilitate the dating of other small finds discovered. These finds also confirm some of the previously proposed hypotheses. The older numismatic find was discovered in layer SU 1039 in quadrant F3. This is a silver denar issued under Venetian Doge Orio Malipiero who ruled from 1178 to 1192 (Diameter 13 mm. Denar; Obv: + AVRIO DVX. Cross in circle; Rev: + S. MARCVS. Cross in circle). The second numismatic find is of somewhat later origin, but exceptionally interesting considering that it was found in burnt layer SU 1037. This is a silver denar issued under Aquileian patriarch Gregorio di Montelongo, who ruled from 1251 to 1269 (Diameter 20 mm. Denar; Obv: .GREGO RIV'.PA. Patriarch sitting facing forward, bishop's staff in right hand, book in left hand; Rev: .AQVI LEGIA. Eagle with lowered wings and head facing right).

The period of his reign is, therefore, the *terminus ante quem non* of this layer and very likely corresponds to a destructive act the fortification was subjected to. A denar issued by an Aquileian patriarch corresponds very well with the hypothesis concerning the identification of the cited layer as the remains of the violent demolition of the fortification in the conflict between Aquileian patriarch and his allies on one side, and Kopar, Count of Gorizia and their allies on the other side, that took place from

1267 till 1274. As historical sources confirm, Conon of Momjan, the Count of Gorica and the people of Kopar succeeded in capturing the fortification and killing the brothers Carsteman and Henry Petrapilosa, in the course of which the fortification itself suffered some demolition (Darovec 2016, 10).

The following stratigraphic unit, SU 1027, yielded ware largely similar to the previous layer. It should be emphasised that the basic difference between these two layers lies in the fact that layer SU 1027 yielded very little of the glazed ware (Fig. 8.6: SJ 1027; Fig. 8.7: 9–11) that, based on parallels, can be dated to the period of the 13th and 14th centuries (Gelichi 1986, 133; Gelichi 1988a, 10, 14, 15; Bradara 2006, 21; Gusar 2010, 40–41, 54, 114–123). Coarse cooking ware is significantly more represented, primarily globular pots that can, based on the form of their rims, be classified into the same dating range (Stadler 1995, cat. A22–A28, A32–A34; Jarnej 2001, 466; Predovnik 2003, 59; Gutjahr & Tiefengraber 2004, 450–455; Bekić 2006, 36–37, T. 2: 10–15).

The following, in terms of chronology, are finds gathered in layers immediately above the occupational layers from the final phases of the utilisation of the fortification. In layers SU 1001, 1010 and 1012 sherds of globular pots of coarse fabric with a thickened rim profile can be found, the likes of which appear in the broader Central European area in the 15th and 16th centuries (Stadler 1995, cat. A22–A28, A32–A34; Jarnej 2001,

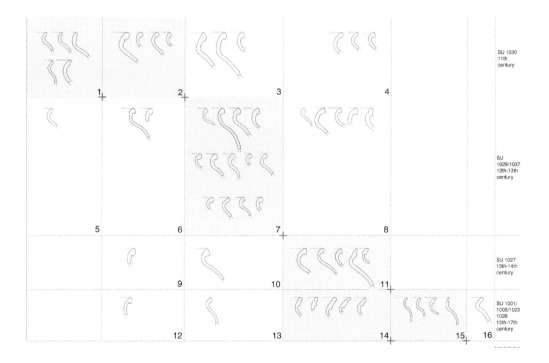

Fig. 8.7: The typological classification of cooking ware rims from layers researched in the palace area

466; Predovnik 2003, 58). Well represented along with coarse cooking ware is more luxurious tableware. This is glazed ware, for the most part imported from northern Italy. All of this ware can be dated to the period from the early 15th to mid-16th century, coming from the direction of Veneto and Emilia-Romagna (Gardelli 1986, 99; Gelichi 1986; 1988, 96; Bojani 1997, 3; Munarini 1998, 17; Gusar 2010, 69, 77, 99, 124, 132) – not surprising given the geopolitical situation of the period.

The youngest sherds of ceramic ware were found in layers mixed primarily with collapsed construction material, i.e. layers that evidently correspond to the period that preceded the final abandonment of the fortification. This group comprises layers SU 1026, 1001, 1005 and 1023. Once again predominant among the coarse cooking ware are sherds of globular pots of coarse fabric with multiple-contoured rim profiles. One novelty does, however, appear. Potsherds of hard fabric with very little temper are also very numerous here, most often with exceptionally thin walls (Višnjić 2012a, 145, T4: 7, 8). Luxurious, glazed ware, that can be dated to the second half of the 16th and early 17th centuries, does, however, constitute a significantly more numerous group (Nepoti 1992, 360; Gelichi & Librenti 1998, 61; Zagarčanin 2004, 52–53; Zglav Martinac 2004, 72–77; Bradara & Saccardo 2007, 33–34, 36; Gusar 2010, 62–63, 103, 168, 180).

Besides the described ceramic sherds there are, of course, numerous small archaeological finds manufactured of other materials, including fragments of glassware, fragments of iron implements and weapons, bronze artefacts that served as items of apparel and so forth. All of the cited artefacts were gathered through the entire stratigraphic sequence.

The architectural development of the structure

Along with the archaeological research, analyses of preserved standing structures were conducted (Fig. 8.8). All of the data presented illustrates just how lengthy and intensive the process of the creation and development of this fortification was, a process that synthesises both the stages of growth and development and of episodes of destruction or degradation. The traces of various processes have been recorded in the well-preserved walls of the architectural complex. 13 phases were identified in the course of the analyses conducted.

To better understand the development process at Petrapilosa it is necessary to touch upon all the data pertaining to the structure available in the historical sources. Although sparse, they do speak in very rough outlines of moments in its past and are, as such, critical to the subsequent interpretation of the architecture and of individual traces that time and the attendant processes have imprinted on the building.

Although the appearance of Petrapilosa is never discussed in the documents that mention its owners, noteworthy data in a number of these documents that speak to the subject of this paper can be found. The oldest data concerning the actual structure are associated with the second half of the 13th century. In 1267, during a time of heightened conflict between the patriarch and his adherents, which include Petrapilosa, against the count of Gorica and his allies, the brothers Carsteman and

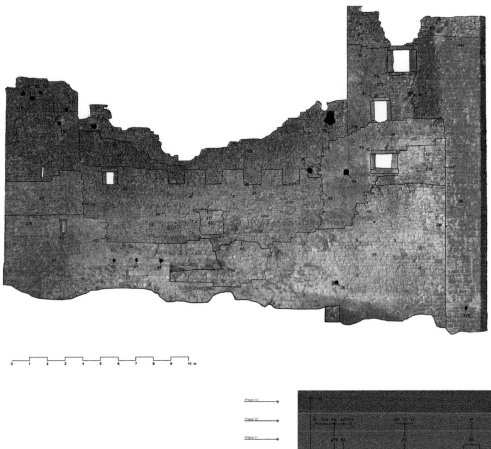

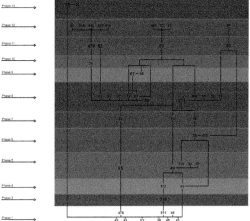

Fig. 8.8: The stratigraphy of the northern wall of the interior of the fortification with the accompanying Harris matrix

Henry Petrapilosa killed Bianquino, the lord of Momjan, (Darovec 1996, 27). Not long thereafter, in 1274, Conon, the brother of the deceased, aided by the count of Gorica and the inhabitants of Kopar, succeeded in capturing the fortress, demolishing it and killing the brothers Carsteman and Henry (CDI 2 1986, 289–604; Klen 1976, 31). By 1285 the fortress had been rebuilt. This is borne out by the fact that the document whereby Vikard II Petrapilosa surrendered Salež castle to the Patriarch as compensation is issued in Petrapilosa (CDI 2 1986, 735–736).

A datum from 1395 speaks of the poor condition of the fortification and of the need for repairs (Minotto 1888, 288–289). These repairs were made five years later when the patriarch Antonio Caetani instructed the marquis Venceslao di Spilimbergo to renovate the palace, roof, thresholds, horse stable and fireplaces in the fortification he had granted him (Paschini 1930, 117). The debate in the Venetian senate on the future of Petrapilosa following its capture in 1421 included proposals for the demolition of the fortification. Four years later its fate was again on the agenda. Demolition was once again tabled as an option given that the castle was run down and not suitable for defence (Darovec 1996, 47). The most recent news is from 1646. In that year Dr Giuseppe Gravisi indicated he was willing to repair the demolished fortification at his own expense. The assessment of the commission that toured Petrapilosa was that, repaired, it could still serve for defensive purposes, and it instructed that the necessary weaponry and ammunition be delivered to the Gravisi family (Senato Mare 1899, 71–72). It appears, however, that the reconstruction was never undertaken.

Archaeological investigation has shown that the construction of the initial fortification can be placed in the late 11th or early 12th century, a period during which the landholding likely passed into the hands of the Aquileian patriarch. This phase can be associated with the erection of the initial, simple defensive structure that, judging from the preserved remains, assumed primarily the utilitarian mission of monitoring and controlling the nearby major communication routes and the possible thwarting of the expansion of the territories of the nearby urban communes into the interior. In this period Petrapilosa was a simple defensive structure formed on the highest point of an elevation, surrounded by simple ramparts of polygonal layout adapted to the available space (Fig. 8.9).

The period of the intensive formation of fortifications – *incastellamento* (encastellation) – is associated with the 10th century when they begin to appear in written sources, as confirmed by archaeological investigation (Vismara 1972, 145; Piuzzi 2000, 133; Settia 2007, 332). This pertains to nearby northern Italy (Piuzzi 2000, 133)

Fig. 8.9: A conceptual reconstruction of the fortification in its first phase of development

but is also applicable to the situation in Istria. Some of the Istrian fortifications are, namely, mentioned for the first time in the course of the 10th century. Thus, in Otto II's donation to the church in Poreč issued in 983 the castle in Pazin, Tar and Nigrinjan (Nigrignanum) are mentioned. In the century that followed there is a significant rise in the number of fortifications mentioned, this being most often associated with the activity of the first Istrian margrave Ulrich I of the Weimar-Orlamünde line in the mid-11th century, which saw him bolster the defences of his frontier march (Bertoša 2003, 132; Darovec 2007, 61). The construction of Petrapilosa in the 11th century is entirely consistent with these processes, but also indicates that the stimuli for the erection of fortifications in this period where significantly more complex than was previously though, i.e. that the motives for construction were not associated solely with the central authority, rather that consideration was also given at lower levels of the feudal social structure to the protection and control of areas under their control.

All of the previous structures are retained in the phase of development that followed, with a tower of rectangular layout added to the western corner of the complex, at the point most exposed to attack (Fig. 8.10). Preserved grooves for the insertion of beams indicate that this first phase had at least three levels. With foundations on a position somewhat more elevated than the rest of the fortification it appears as a taller structure. Based on the preserved ruins it appears not to have had any openings on the western and northwestern walls, with defensive efforts launched from the tops of the walls. Light most likely entered the interior of the tower from the south side, well secured by the cliff face beneath it, as is borne out by a small window in the preserved first phase ground level wall section. There may also have been openings on the eastern wall facing the courtyard from which the tower was accessed. Further to the east the walls of the first phase of development are made higher. A small structure was adjoined to the tower and to the outer northeastern wall. Its existence is confirmed by traces on the northern wall of what was most likely a gable roof. The building had two levels. The grooves that once took the beams point to the likely presence of a guard path running on from here.

Additional structures were erected in the interior of the fortification in the course of the third phase of its development. Only a part of the walls subsequently

Fig. 8.10: A conceptual reconstruction of the fortification in its second phase of development

Fig. 8.11: A conceptual reconstruction of the fortification in its third phase of development

incorporated into the eastern wall of the palace are preserved. Little more can, therefore, be said of their appearance. The same period saw the construction to the east of the main portal of a building that essentially constitutes the first phase of the formation of an outer courtyard. Also built during this period was a church dedicated to St Mary Magdalene with its underpinning wall (Fig. 8.11). As all this content is very much characteristic of medieval feudal fortifications, almost unimaginable without them, their construction can be associated with the appearance of the aristocratic *de Petrapilosa* family, which held this estate as a fief from the early 13th century. The erection of the tower should, then, be associated with the manifestation of the privileged status of an owner of a fief. The other cited content was likely built not long afterwards.

The technique employed in the construction of the walls of this phase raises certain doubts as to this early dating. They were built employing a specific method in which the faces of the walls are formed of regular dressed stone blocks laid in courses of unequal height, while the interior of the wall is built in the *opus spicatum* technique. This technique can be found at much more recently erected walls, for example at Medvedgrad, Modruš, Blagaj na Korani or at Hrastovica. The erection of all these structures is dated to the second half of the 13th or early 14th century (Horvat, 1986, 183). Nevertheless, the position of the walls built using this technique in the stratigraphic sequences identified at Petrapilosa support the older dating, i.e. as has already been pointed out they are likely not more recent than the early 13th century.

St Mary Magdalene church, forming an integral part of the outer ramparts, is of irregular quadrilateral layout with an inscribed quadrilateral barrel-vaulted apse. Churches with these characteristics are numbered among Romanesque structures (Marušić 1974, 22; Šonje 1982, 131), and it has been dated previously to the period from the 11th to early 13th century (Mihovilić 2000, 25; Krnjak 2003, 14; Bradara 2006, 46). The disposition of this building within the relative-chronological sequence of the Petrapilosa fortification and the proposed dating of the other elements to about the same period, places the erection of the church in the first half of the 13th century.

The most precise datum provided by the previously cited documents is the demolition that took place between 1267 and 1274 (CDI 2 1986, 289–604; Klen, 1976, 31). Two phases

Fig. 8.12: A conceptual reconstruction of the fortification in its fifth phase of development

of destruction identified on the walls of Petrapilosa can be associated with this event (Phases 4 and 7). Following the first demolition of phase four there was significant construction. This saw the significant expansion of the initial palace. Although it is hard to believe that a destructive act in which the two leading members of the family are killed would spark the construction of a large residential palace, the period that followed nevertheless sees the Petrapilosa house retain its significance and its two subsequent leaders playing key roles in local events in Istria and Friuli in the last quarter of the 13th and first half of the 14th century.

The fifth phase of development sees the repair of structures in the course of the rebuilding of the northern wall of the fortification. This phase also likely saw the erection of a building with a floor plan occupying the entire area of the palace that fused several older buildings. This building had three storeys. The same period also saw the partial westward expansion of the outer courtyard by the extension of the platform on which the church was positioned and the forming of a narrow passage along the northern wall of the central body of the fortification (Fig. 8.12).

In the sixth phase of development the fortification was reinforced with a thickening of the existing walls to the western and northwestern sides (the *schildmauer*). The new wall was built on to the outer face of the tower walls attaining its existing height and continuing on at the same level. Thus, now, the western and northwestern walls had a thickness of 4 m and a maximum height of 19 m, while the next 4.5 m of the northern wall had the same height, but the thickness of the older wall (Fig. 8.13). The tower retained its function, significantly bolstered by the new wall at the most accessible part of the fortification – the point most threatened by enemy attack. Grooves for beams and traces of openings at the very top of the outer northwestern wall indicate the possibility that there was a wooden structure here used for defensive purposes. The subsequent demolitions make it difficult to ascertain with certainty how far this wall ran further to the east. It was most likely not much farther from the point to which it is presently preserved. Steps led from the newly formed platform at the top of the wall to the tower, the only point from which the platform was accessible.

The demolition from the period between 1267 and 1274 should, then, be taken as associated with the fourth phase, and the construction of phases five and six

Josip Višnjić

Fig. 8.13: A conceptual reconstruction of the fortification in its sixth phase of development

with the activity of Vikard II Petrapilosa. Further corroboration can be found in the erection of the *schildmauer* characteristic of Germanic areas in the 13th and 14th centuries (Antonow 1977). The construction of the shield wall covering the western and northwestern walls of the tower and the northwestern wall running on from here, producing a wall over 4 m thick and over 18 m tall in places, is linked with the increased use of stone throwing siege engines in the 12th and 13th centuries. These machines, known of in previous periods, saw a developmental breakthrough at the time with the invention of a new siege engine known as the *trabucco* (trebuchet) (Cantor 1999, 48; Piuzzi 2000, 139; Settia 2007, 354). A wall thickness of almost 2 m at this part of the fortification prior to the construction of the second phase was quite sufficient in ensuring defence in the conditions of early medieval warfare. The increased use of siege engines, however, demanded the additional reinforcement of the most exposed sides of fortifications. Given that traces of collapse on these walls cannot be found it is evident that they accomplished their task, with most damage occurring at the northern and eastern walls of the inner courtyard, i.e. the walls that continued on from here.

Identifying stylistic characteristics that could help us in dating the palace is not easy. The only possible clues are the characteristic windows on the northern and eastern walls. These are windows in niches that reach almost to the floor with stone sills. Windows of this type are usually associated with the Gothic period and are known from Ribnik near Karlovac, Kebelj in Slovenia or at Loibersdorf in Lower Austria (Stopar 1977, 128–129; Horvat 1989, 32; Fragner, Krenn & Tuzar 1996). The nearest analogies are found at Possert in northeastern Istria where they can be dated to the second half of 14th century (Višnjić 2012b). These types of window niches do, however, appear earlier, for example at Zagreb's Lotršćak tower in the mid-13th century (Horvat 1997, 44–45), while Piper (1993, 453) notes that these windows appear in the 12th century, become widespread in the 13th and remained in use through to the 15th. These dates are consistent with the presumed dating of the first phase of the palace to the first half of the 13th century.

The concrete data from historical sources for the second demolition, which we can associate with the seventh phase, are not known. It may be associated with one of the many conflicts in which Vikard II and Petar Petrapilosa took part in the course

Fig. 8.14: A conceptual reconstruction of the fortification in its eighth phase of development

of their lives. If, then, phases five and six are associated with the activities that took place immediately post the 1274 event, the repeated demolition likely took place in the early 14th century.

In the eighth phase of development there was a comprehensive renovation of the entire complex. In this period, the palace was raised a further two storeys, attaining the height of the tower. To the north side the palace had three windows, one each on the three upper storeys, just like on the eastern wall. The entrance to the palace was located in the same wall. Because of the safety offered by the high cliff at this section and the suitable exposure to the sun, it is likely that the southern wall of the palace was also perforated with window openings.

The same construction intervention saw the repair of the southern wall of the main tower and the southern wall of the inner courtyard. The two doors preserved in this wall are from this phase. The wall terminated in crenellations. Repairs are effected to the damaged walls terminating in crenellations on the northern and eastern sides. This phase also sees the erection of a tower at the northeastern corner of the inner courtyard.

Also from this phase is a door, later walled up, with an arched lintel located on the northern wall of the inner courtyard. As the outer side was quite high above the level of the terrain it is likely that its function was defensive and that it led to some type of *bretèche* or similar, now destroyed, structure. The window at the level of the crenellations, near the northeastern tower, is also from this phase and permits the hypothesis of the presence of a building at this location. It was this construction intervention that created the outer courtyard in its full form (Fig. 8.14).

The construction of these elements is very likely still associated with the first half of the 14th century, the period in which the Petrapilosa family still plays a significant role in the area. Also, as has already been noted, the palace and horse stable were in need of thorough renovation by the late 14th century (Minotto 1888, 288–289) and it is hard to believe that buildings built not long before that would have already required repair of this kind.

Smaller scale construction that occurred in the following three phases (from 8 to 11) should be placed in the period from the early 15th to late 16th century. These two

Fig. 8.15: A conceptual reconstruction of the fortification in its eleventh phase of development

hundred years primarily saw the extension of existing walls and buildings, with no major construction undertaken. The palace was made taller with a minor heightening of the roof, reducing its pitch. This likely rendered the loft useable for residential purposes. This is also borne out by the fact that, in place of the single previous opening, the side facing the inner courtyard now had two doors and one window. On the exterior side of this wall there is a horizontal series of grooves for affixing beams that may be the traces of a wooden terrace accessed through the cited door.

The main tower was also raised by a full storey, once again becoming dominant in terms of its height in relation to the palace. At about the same time the northern wall of the inner courtyard is also raised to the height of the tower in the northeastern corner, whereby it may have lost its function. The traces of this extension are also visible on the eastern wall. The walling up of the crenellations at the northeastern tower, repairs to the western wall of the main tower and the negating of the terrace on the eastern wall of the palace with the walling up of the door leading to it occurred somewhat later (Fig. 8.15).

It is clear from the above mentioned that the construction of defensive structures that would correspond to the need to defend against the use of gunpowder-fired weapons that saw growing use from the 15th century on was negligible. Only the construction of a small semi-circular tower alongside the main gate into the fortification and some openings for firearms in the western part of the outer courtyard can be associated with these activities. The lack of these structures clearly confirms that all preceding phases were built to respond to medieval military technology, when the height and thickness of walls constituted the chief guarantee of the safety of a defended position.

Phase twelve covers the long period in which the castle gradually deteriorated, reduced from a strong defensive point to the present ruins. This process began with a fire in the 1620s and stretched over almost four centuries, leaving many traces on the walls. The latest thirteenth phase covers the construction interventions that have been made on the architectural remains of Petrapilosa over the past fifteen years.

The example of Petrapilosa shows that archaeological researches and archaeological analytical methods are the most suited, if not the only means of collecting data on the dating, character and appearance of structures that do not offer an abundance of architectural details which would be helpful when dating them. Archaeological researches have also been shown, in cases of this comprehensive conservation intervention, to be an essential project component for collecting data for the most adequate methods for conservation of preserved architectural structures.

Bibliography

Antonow, A. (1977) *Burgen des südwestdeutschen Raums in 13. und 14. Jahrhundert unter besonderer Berücksichtigungder Schildmauer*. Freiburg, Veröffentlichung des Alemannischen Instituts.

Bekić, L. (2006) Stara Ves kod Nedelišća (Čakovec). Višeslojno razvedeno nalazište. In L. Bekić (ed.) *Zaštitna arheološka istraživanja u okolici Varaždina*, 203–248. Zagreb, Ministarstvo kulture RH.

Beltrame, F. & Colussa, S. (2002) Saggio di scavo presso il Castello di Manzano. Nota preliminare. *Archeologia Medievale* XXIX, 45–55.

Benedetti, A. (1964) Gli antichi Signori di Pietrapilosa. *Pagine Istriane*, 12–13.

Benussi, B. (2004) *Nel medio evo. Pagine di storia Istriana*. Fiume, Università Popolare (reprint of original publication published from 1893 till 1897).

Bertoša, M. (2003) Istra od 6. do 10. st, In F. Šanjek (ed.) *Povijest Hrvata. Srednji vijek,* 115–134. Zagreb, Školska knjiga.

Bianchi, J. (1847) *Thesaurus Ecclesiae Aquilejensis. Opus saeculi XIV*. Udine, Typogr. archiep. Trombetti-Murero.

Bojani, G. C. (1997) *Per una storia della ceramica di Faenza - Materiale dalle mura di Portello*. Faenza, Edit Faenza.

Bradara, T. (2006) Nuovi rinvenimenti di cheramica tardomedioevale e rinascimentale in Istria. In M. Guštin, S. Gelichi & K. Spindler (eds.) *The Heritage of the Serenissima*, 45–50. Koper, Založba Annales.

Bradara, T. & Saccardo, F. (2007) *Keramički nalazi iz Rovinja - uvala Valdibora i otok Sv. Katarina*. Katalog izložbe. Rovinj, Zavičajni muzej grada Rovinja.

Cantor, F. C. (ed.) (1999) *The Pimlico encyclopedia of the Middle Ages*. London, Pimlico.

CDI (1986) Kandler, P. *Codice Diplomatico Istriano* (1–5). Trieste, Tipogra fia Riva (reprint of original publication published from 1860 till 1865).

Cetinić, Ž. (1999) *Stranče - Gorica, starohrvatsko groblje*, Pula, Arheološki muzej Istre.

Corbanese, G. G. (1984) *Grande atlante storico - cronologico comparato da G. G. Corbanese. 1. Il Friuli, Trieste e l'Istria dalla preistoria alla caduta del Patriarco d'Aquileia*. Udine, Del Bianco.

Darovec, D. (1996) *Kostel Petrapilosa*. Pazin, Josip Turčinović.

Darovec, D. (2007) *Petrapilosa. Grad, rodbina, fevd in markizat*. Koper, Založba Annales.

De Franceschi, C. (1852) Sulle varie popolazioni dell'Istria. *L'Istria* 7, 233–238.

Ferri, M., Forti, A., Fresia, S., Pluskowski, A., Saccocci, A., Seetah, K. & Vignola, M. (2008) Vita quotidiana a Sacuidic, In S. Gelichi, F. Piuzzi & A. Ciancioci (eds.) *Sauchuidic presso Forni superioore. Ricerche archeologiche in un castello della Carnia*. Udine, Serie dell'insegnamento di Archeologia Medievale.

Flego, I. (2000) Markizi Gravisi iz Petrapilose na Buzeštini. *Buzetski zbornik* 27, 35–54.

Fragner, B., Krenn, M. & Tuzar, T. (1996) Bauaufnahmen an der ehemaligen Burganlage in der KG Loibersdorf, Niderösterreich. *Fundberichte aus Österreich* 35, 238–252.

Gardelli, G. (1986) *Ceramiche del Medioevo e del Rinascinamento*. Ferara, Belriguardo.

Gelichi, S. (1986) Studi sulla ceramica medievale rimanese, 2. Il complesso dell'ex Hotel Commercio. *Archeologia Medievale* 13, 117–172.

Gelichi, S. (1988) La maiolica italiana della prioma meta del XV secolo. La produzione in Emilia-Romagna e i problemi della cronologia. *Archeologia Medievale* XV, 85–104.

Gelichi, S. & Librenti, M. (1998) *Senza immensa dote. Le Clarisse a Finale emilia tra archaeologia e soria*. Firenze, Serie dell'insegnamento di Archeologia Medievale.

Gusar, K. (2010) *Kasnosrednjovjekovna i novovjekovna glazirana keramika na širem zadarskom području*. Doktorski rad, Sveučilište u Zadru, Filozofski fakultet.

Gutjahr, C. & Tiefengraber, G. (2004) Die mittelalterliche Wahranlage "Turmbauerkogel" bei Eibiswald (Ivnik), Bez. Deutschlandsberg, Weststeiermark. *Arheološki vestnik* 55, 439–480.

Horvat, Z. (1986) O izgledu srednjovjekovnog zida na primjerima nekih građevina u kontinentalnoj Hrvatskoj. *Godišnjak zaštite spomenika kulture Hrvatske* 12, 179–191.

Horvat, Z. (1989) *Strukture gotičke arhitekture*. Zagreb, Društvo povjesničara umjetnosti SR Hrvatske, XLVII.

Horvat, Z. (1997) Prozori na burgovima XIII – XV. st. u kontinentalnoj Hrvatskoj. *Prostor* 5 (1/13), 42–60.

Jarnej, R. (2001) Ausgewählte mittelalterliche Keramik aus Magdalensberg – Gipfelgrabung. In F. Wilhelm Leitner, G. Piccottini (eds.) *Carinthia romana und die römische Welt*, 465–469.

Kandler, P. (1875) *Notizie storiche di Montona*. Trieste, Tipografia del Lloyd austriaco.

Kirac, L. (1990) *Crtice iz istarske povijesti*. Pazin, Josip Turčinović (reprint of original publication published from 1949).

Klen, D. (1977) Iz prošlosti Kostela – Petra Pilose i njegovih sela. *Buzetski zbornik* 2, 29–50.

Kos, F. (1928) *Gradivo za zgodovino Slovencev v srednjem veku* 5. Ljubljana, Leonova družba.

Krnjak, O. (2003) *Kostel Petrapilosa. O tragovima fresaka iz crkvice Sv. Marije Magdalene*. Pula, Arheološki muzej Istre.

Marušić, B. (1971) Kompleks bazilike Sv. Sofije u Dvogradu. *Histria Archaeologica* 2 (2). Pula.

Marušić, B. (1974) Istarska grupa spomenika sakralne arhitekture s upisanom apsidom. *Histria Archaeologica* 3 (1). Pula.

Mihovilić, K. (2000) Arheološka istraživanje crkve Sv. Marije Magdalene u Petrapilosi. *Buzetski zbornik* 27, 20–33.

Minotto, A. S. (1887–1900) Senato Misti (cose dell'Istria). *Atti e memorie della societa' Istriana di archeologia e storia patria* (3–6). Parenzo.

Munarini, M. (1998) Origini e diffusione della ceramica graffita tra Alto e Basso Medioevo, In R. Magnani and M. Munarini (eds.) *La ceramica graffita del Rinascimento tra Po, Adige e Oglio*, 11–25. Ferrara, Belriguardo.

Negri, A. (2007) La ceramica grezza. In F. Piuzzi (ed.) *Il pozzeto USM 438. Uno squarzio di vita quotidiana nel XIII secolo*, 29–52. Gradisca d'Isonzo, Accademia Jaufre Rudel.

Nepoti, S. (1992) La ceramiche a Ferrara nel Rinascimento: i reperti da corso della Giovecca, In S. Gelichi (ed.) *Ferrara primo e dopo il Castello*, 289–366. Ferrara, Spazio libri editori.

Paschini, P. (1930) L'Istria patriarcale durante il governo del patriarca Antonio Caetani (1395–1402). *Atti e memorie della societa' Istriana di archeologia e storia patria* 42, 87–119.

Piuzzi, F. (2000) Contributi per lo studio dell'incastellamento nel nord-est Italiano. Le strutture protofeudali alla luce di recenti dati archeologici (IX–XII secolo). In G. P. Brogiolo (ed.) *Congresso Nazionale di Archeologia Medievale* 2, 132–143. Brescia.

Piuzzi F., Di Mateo, S., Cossio, S., Marchese, G., Putano, F., Brancati, C., Mazzei, M. & Vignola, M. (2003) La sequenza periodizzata delle fasi identificate (anni 1997.'99/2001-'02), In F. Piuzzi (ed.) *Progetto Castello della Motta di Savorgnano*, 37–126. Firenze, All'insegna del Giglio.

Piper, O. (1993) *Burgenkunde*. Augsburg, Weltbild Verlag (reprint of original publication published in 1912.).

Predovnik, K. (2003) *Trdnjava Kostanjevica na Starem gradu nad Podbočjem*. Ljubljana, Archaeologia historica Slovenica.

Rigoni, A. N. (1992) Indagini archeologice nell'area della fortificazine medievale di Castelciés (Cavaso del Tomba). *Quaderni di archeologia del Veneto* 8, 60–69.

Senato Mare (1893–1899) *Atti e memorie della societa' Istriana di archeologia e storia patria* IX–XV. Parenzo.

Settia, A. A. (2007) Utvrde, naseljavanje i rat. In E. Cravetto (ed.) *Povijest 6. Rani i razvijeni srednji vijek*, 324–357. Piotello, Biblioteka Jutanjeg lista.

Sirk, Ž. (2002) Između lava i orla (I): srednjovijekovni gradovi, kašteli i kule Istre i Hrvatskog primorja i njihovi gospodari. *Nova Istra* 21 (2–3), 171–224.

Stadler, H. (1995) Ausgrabungen auf der Burgruine Flaschberg bei Oberdrauburg in Kärnten. *Nearchos* 3, 137–334.

Stopar, I. (1977) *Razvoj grajske arhitekture na Slovenskem Štajerskem*. Ljubljana, Slovenska matica.

Šonje, A. (1982) *Crkvena arhitektura zapadne Istre*. Zagreb – Pazin, Kršćanska sadašnjost.

Terrier, J., Jurković, M., Matejčić, I. & Ruffieux, P. (2007) Les fouilles archéologiques de Guran en Istrie (Croatie) en 2005 et 2006. *Genava* LV, 271–321.

Villa, L. (2004) L'area friuliana. In S. Patitucci Uggeri (ed.) *La ceramica altomedievale in Italia*, 79–91. Firenze, All'Insegna del Giglio.

Vismara, G. (1972) La disciplina giuridica del castello dell'alto medioevo. *Studia et Documenta Historiae et Iuris* 38, 137–148.

Višnjić, J. (2012a) Rezultati arheoloških istraživanja provedenih unutar kaštela Petrapilosa tijekom 2010. i 2011. g. *Buzetski zbornik* 39, 123–158.

Višnjić, J. (2012b) Srednjovjekovna utvrda Possert. Šest godina arheoloških radova i konzervatorsko-restauratorskih zahvata na sačuvanim arhitektonskim strukturama. *Histria archaeologica* 43, 67–154.

Zagarčanin, M. (2004) *Stari Bar. Keramika venecijanskog doba*. Koper, Založba Annales.

Zglav Martinac, H. (2004) *Ulomak do ulomka... Prilog proučavanju keramike XIII. - XVIII. stoljeća iz Dioklecijanove palače u Splitu*. Split, Književni krug.

Chapter 9

The formation of the three-compartment rural house in medieval Central Europe as a cultural synthesis of different building traditions

Pavel Vařeka

Introduction

The three-compartment rural house was introduced in eastern Central Europe as early as the later Middle Ages and it remained the most common type of traditional village house until the 20th century. Archaeological, ethnological, historical and linguistic research of this type of vernacular house has achieved extensive results over the last hundred years in terms of gaining detailed knowledge of regional variants, internal functional structure, and developmental transformations; nevertheless, the formation of the three-compartment house remains unclear. This paper examines the earliest material evidence of this house type, compares its attributes, discusses the possibilities of its formation process, and seeks to assess its social and cultural significance within the frame of the long-term development of the rural built environment in Central Europe.

The three-compartment rural house is defined by its built-up form with a rectangular ground plan, spatial composition of functionally distinct components combining living quarter with the livestock and/or storage under the same roof, and a consistent access and passage structure. The designation of 'tripartite' does not refer to the number of rooms, but to the concept of three zones that have different functions and may consist of more components (e.g. Pražák 1958; Frolec 1982; Bedal 1993, 89–92; Smetánka 1994). The central entrance area is represented by a corridor, which works as a traffic zone giving access to other parts of the house, but may be also used for other purposes. The living core of the house is situated on one side, with the only heated room used for daily living. The third part, which is used for economic activities connected with farming, is placed on the other side. Its main function is determined by two sub-types of the three-compartment house: a) a *Wohnstahlhaus* (German) or *chlévní dům* (Czech; byre-house) with a byre which can be entered both from inside the house through the corridor and from the yard via a separate door and b) a *Wohnspeicharhaus*

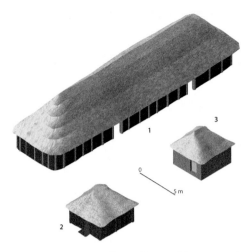

Fig. 9.1: Comparison of house forms of the Germanic (1) and Slavic (2-3) building tradition. 1. A large Germanic byre house accommodating both dwelling and economic functions under the same roof 2-3. Sunken and surface small one-compartment dwelling house of the Slavic world (Malina & Vařeka 2018)

or *špýcharový/komorový dům* (granary/storage-house) with a granary, or a storage room. The central corridor of the granary-house provides the only access to the house via the entrance leading to a yard, whereas the byre-house has an additional entrance to a byre from the outside. There are many variants of the basic tripartite concept connecting dwelling and economic functions under the same roof on each side of the corridor defined by an extension of the basic linear scheme by additional parts on both a longitudinal (two or three aisles and more bays on both sides) and vertical axis (cellars and storey) (Niederle 1913, 758–779; Pražák 1958; Baumgarten 1980, 53–64; Bedal 1993, 89–92).

Different Early Medieval building traditions

Archaeological evidence of Early Medieval settlements and their built environment in Central Europe is in nearly all cases based on excavations of sites situated in areas which have been used as arable land for a long period of time. Therefore, a significant part of the archaeological context is missing, i.e. cultural layers above the subsoil, original terrain level, house floors, evidence of artefact distribution, etc. The archaeological record includes only indirect evidence of surface buildings represented by features set to the subsoil as post-holes or grooves, while some constructions did not leave any traces in the ground at all, e.g. corner-timbering or sill beams without deeper bedding trenches. On the other hand, sunken houses or their parts are well preserved, however their original depth can be only estimated. Hence the interpretation of Early Medieval rural architectural remains is very limited and reconstructions are hypothetical (Vařeka 1991; 2004, 22–25).

Farms in Early Medieval Germany were made up of irregular clusters of several buildings with limited archaeological evidence of fences and ditches marking their areas. The main post-built house accommodating both peasant family and livestock was surrounded with smaller buildings for storage and production activities such as sunken houses, granaries, haystacks but also storage pits. Rural houses differ in northwestern and southern Germany. Longhouses in the north consisted of a living part equipped with a central hearth, an entrance part, and a large byre derived from an old tradition of three-aisled longhouses going back to the Bronze Age. Rural houses underwent several changes during the early Middle Ages regarding wall constructions, roofing techniques, internal framework layout, and a ground plan form. Farm houses in southern Germany are generally smaller (mostly 50–100 m^2) with a variety of ground plans, usually one-aisled and two-aisled houses, in some cases with additional side wings (Zimmermann 1998; Schreg 2002, 114–115; 2012, 253–260).

The more or less eastern and northeastern part of Central Europe includes areas of the Slavic cultural tradition of Bohemia and Moravia, Poland, Slovakia, northeastern Germany, parts of central Germany, northeastern Bavaria, Austria and also Hungary (e.g. Herrmann 1981; Dušek 1983; Lecziejewicz 1989; Gringmuth-Dallmer 1999; Losert 2012), which provide archaeological evidence of a very different Early Medieval building tradition. Since the late 6th century, dwellings were represented by small one-compartment sunken buildings (usually less than 20 m^2) of a square plan equipped with a stone or clay oven placed in a corner. Wall constructions were corner-timbered or post-built, wattle-and-daub or sunken-and-grooved construction. Main regional differences can be seen in the distribution of sunken and surface houses, the latter of which are concentrated in the north where significant sunken houses are not present. An important developmental trend is characterised by gradual substitution of sunken houses for surface houses during the 10th–12th/13th centuries and some changes have been also seen in house size. There is some evidence indicating that, in some cases, a second part may have been annexed to the one-compartment house, which served as an entrance room in the later Early Medieval period. Knowledge of the Early Medieval Slavic farms is very limited due to the absence of surface archaeological contexts on most sites. Except for sunken houses archaeological excavations document numerous storage pits, including typical pear-shaped grain silos and surface outhouses of some kind. Compared to western Central Europe, the situation is even more complicated due to the absence of distinctive surface buildings with thick load-bearing posts set deeply into the subsoil. The widespread use of the block-building technique is presumed which does not leave traces in the subsoil level (Donat 1980; Chudziak 1987; Moździoch 1996; Takács 1998; 2002; Šaľkovský 2001; Ruttkay 2002; Vařeka 2004, 229–237; Buko 2006, 298–301). Using ethnological analogies, some later medieval villages and rare Early Medieval sites with preserved stratigraphy, we assume that the core of archaic Slavic farms may have been formed by a pair of two small one-compartment square-plan buildings situated diagonally opposite one another: a dwelling house and a storage house (Niederle 1913, 748–774; Moszyński 1929, 536–558; Meduna 1992; Belcredi 2006, 287–290; Vařeka et al. 2011, 333–334). Neighbouring nomadic building tradition of the eastern European steppes, represented by remains of circular yurt-dwellings, has been only very rarely documented in Carpathian basin where it was connected with Early Medieval Hungarian culture (Takácz 2002, 282; Molnár 2011, 674–677).

The earliest three-compartment rural houses in Central Europe

Archaeological research of high to Late Medieval rural sites in Central Europe has documented the extensive transformation of the Early Medieval building tradition during the 12th–14th centuries. An important change in rural housing is characterised by the adaptation of stone foundations, which in southern and central Germany are dated to the 12th–13th centuries corresponding with the introduction of timber-farming, which replaced earlier earth-fastened post constructions (Donat 1995, 427; Schreg 2002, 116–118). In eastern Central Europe this innovation can be dated to the late 13th and 14th century, however the character of widespread block construction did not change (Vařeka 2004, 238–239, 263, 274–275, 288–289). Another innovation can be seen in rectangular cellars with wooden or stone revetments and sunken staircases, which may represent the sunken parts of the unpreserved surface multi-compartment houses. The introduction of cellars in the rural milieu is dated to the 13th century in central and southern Germany (Donat 1993, 22–226; 1995, 427; Kenzler 2002, 103–104; Scherg 2002, 116–118), as well as in some parts of eastern Central Europe (Parádi 1979; Ruttkay 1998, 63; Pálóczi-Horváth 2002, 312-317; Ruttkay 2002, 269–270; Vařeka 2004, 261–263).

Later medieval village excavations in southern, central and eastern Germany produced a number of rural house remains including several complete ground plans. Only a few of them might be interpreted as buildings with a three-compartment layout (Rückert 1988; Gommerstedt, building 23 – Timpel 1982, 33; Donat 1995, 430–432; Oberstetten – Schmidt 1986; Donat 1995, 433; Schönfeld – Fehring 1973; Fig. 9.2: 1); others have more differentiated ground plans or may represent two-compartment buildings. Therefore, it is difficult to find well-dated archaeological evidence demonstrating the origins of the new three-compartment house type. Transformation of the Early Medieval building tradition with post-built houses into timber-framed buildings having both living and important economic functions under the same roof equipped with stone foundations appears to have taken place during the late 12th and 13th century. Evidence of innovation in heating is indicated by several finds of oven remains situated in what were very likely living rooms (e.g. Gommerstedt, building 23 – Timpel 1982, 33; Stahlnheim – Ernst & Klápště 1993). Thanks to intensive building archaeology research, a large number of preserved standing farmhouses have been detected in southern Germany that date to the late 14th and 15th century, significantly supplementing archaeological sources. Houses with a three-compartment structure can be divided into several variants according to longitudinal and transverse spatial division and the function of individual rooms (Bedal 1993, 89–91; 1998, 115–118). The central part is always formed by a corridor providing access to side areas which can be divided into two or three bays forming *Neunrraster* (ninefold or six-room pattern) or *Sechsrraster* (sixfold or nine-room pattern) pattern (Bedal 2002, 253). The *Stube* (living section), usually situated in the southeastern corner of the house, has a sunken-and-grooved construction (horizontal timbers set to four corner posts) with outer daub plaster and a panelled ceiling providing a small (4 × 4–5 × 5 m) but very well-insulated room. A comfortable smoke-free heating system was created by a

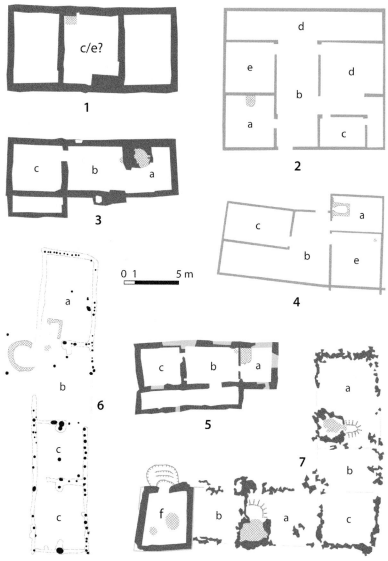

Fig. 9.2: Three-compartment houses in Central Europe in the 13th to 15th century. 1. Oberstetten (Baden-Württemberg, Germany). House with probably a central entrance part/kitchen, living room and byre/storage room; presumably 13th century (Schmidt 1986) 2. Höfstetten (Bayern, Germany). Preserved timber rural house dated to 1367/1368. (Bedal 1998) 3, 5. Hard (Ober Österreich, Austria). Houses from the late 13th and 14th century (Felgenhauer-Schmiedt 2008) 4. St Ulrich (Byern). Preserved corner-timbered house from the 14th century (1329-1379; Kirchener & Kirchner 1998) 6. Szentkirály (eastern Hungary). Post-built house with extended backing oven, 15th and early 16th century (Pálóczi-Horváth 1990) 7. Sarvaly (western Hungary). Two connected houses from the 14th to early 16th century; open hearths situated in the sunken part (f) may indicate heating of the supposed wine cellar during cold winters. (Holl & Parádi 1982) a. entrance room b. living room provided with a heating equipment (oven/tile stove) c. granary/storage room d. byre e. black kitchen f. cellar (lower storage room), black – post holes, dark grey – stone foundations, light grey – timber constructions (preserved buildings), crosswise – heating equipment (Malina & Vařeka 2018)

tile-stove serviced from an adjacent 'black' kitchen. Houses had no chimneys, so the smoke escaped through the inside of the house and the roof (Bedal 1998, 104–113, 118–123; for the origins and dissemination of the *Stube* see Atzbach 2014). Other parts of the house were used as byres and storage rooms (Fig. 9.2: 2). Wall constructions were timber-framed, often with internal load-bearing posts (two or three aisles), but stone-built houses were also used in some regions, as well as corner-timbered log houses in the Alps (Fig. 9.2: 4). Direct predecessors of later types of vernacular houses can be found among standing Late Medieval rural buildings as the most widespread three-compartment byre-house (Bedal 1993, 115–116; 1998, 104–113, 115–123; 2002, 252–255).

In eastern Central Europe, archaic one-compartment houses remained in use in some regions until the end of the Middle Ages in addition to two-compartment buildings that started to appear already in the later phase of the early Middle Ages (Páloczy-Horváth 2002, 308–312; Vařeka 2004, 258–259, 275–278; Belcredi 2006, 284–295; Vařeka *et al.* 2011, 333–334). In addition, three-compartment houses with differentiated house plans consisting of a living area, central corridor and a storage area were adopted, showing the introduction of the multi-functional rural house with both dwelling and economic functions under the same roof. Archaeological excavations have so far revealed the earliest evidence of the three-compartment houses in Bohemia and Moravia, Austria, and Hungary, which date to the late 13th and 14th century.

The largest data set regarding the late 13th–15th century village built environment, including nearly 50 excavated three-compartment houses, has been produced by field research in Bohemia and Moravia (Šaurová 1973; 1977; Nekuda 1975; Smetánka 1988; Měchurová 1997; Nekuda & Nekuda 1997; Vařeka 2004, 259–261; Klír 2016). In addition to the investigation of deserted villages, the medieval rural research programme in the Czech Republic has also included the examination of the medieval cores of existing villages using opportunities provided by rescue archaeology, however documented three-compartment houses are only fragmentarily preserved (Nováček & Vařeka 1996; Vařeka *et al.* 2010; Vařeka 2013). Building archaeology research has revealed a gradually increasing number of preserved block houses dendro-dated to the 1490s and 16th century and also a stone-built rural architecture which can be chronologically classified to the same period using architectural late-gothic details such as portals and windows (Škabrada 1992; 2003, 15–25, 100–102).

The introduction of three-compartment houses in Bohemia and Moravia can be dated to the late 13th and early 14th century, representing the most numerous type of house, which, in addition to one-compartment and two-compartment houses, was in use until the 15th century. Archaeological evidence mostly provides information about the ground plan level of the house. The size of excavated three-compartment houses in Bohemia and Moravia dated to the late 13th–15th century ranges from 5 × 15 m to 11 × 22 m. Houses had log walls set on stone foundations, but some were partly or even completely built of clay-bound stones. The most important facility of the house is a large stone oven with an open hearth in front of its opening, which was situated in a corner next to the door of the living area. Only very few finds indicate the placement of another hearth in the back part of the corridor. In many cases, the storage area has a sub-terrain section accessible by a sunken-staircase. Floors of corridors and storage areas were stone-paved and living areas had clay floors. Numerous finds of locks and keys demonstrate the locking of house doors, especially in storage areas. Dwelling houses are in nearly all cases gable-oriented, using one side of the yard which was lined on one or more sides by outhouses as byres, stables, granaries and barns (Vařeka 2004, 256–264).

Based on the analysis of formal attributes, the prevailing granary/storage-house can be divided into three variants (Fig. 9.3): 1) house with a linear scheme ground plan, 2) house with a differentiated ground plan with two aisles, and 3) 'L'-shaped house (Smetánka 1994, 118–124; Vařeka 2004, 259–261). The most widespread variant 1 is formed by three parts of roughly the same size – a *síň* (central corridor) which provided access to a *jizba* (living room) on one side and a *komora* (storage room) on the other. In some cases, the storage area consists of a lower room sunken partly into the ground, serving as a cellar, and an upper room representing a storey. Further parts may have been annexed to the three-compartment core of the house on both sides, including additional storage rooms and byres, however these parts were always given separate entrances to a yard and had no direct access to the house-core. Houses of the second variant are longitudinally divided into a main and a narrow side aisle which provided additional small rooms. The third variant differs from the first one only by its angular house plan. Only one example of a byre-house might be represented by a house excavated in the deserted village of Spindelbach in northwest Bohemia near the border with Saxony. Both the living and possible byre area seem to be divided into two aisles (Klír 2016).

The upper parts of the Late Medieval village house in Bohemia can be reconstructed using standing buildings, especially the *jizba*, which was most commonly preserved (e.g. Škabrada 1992; 2003, 18–22; Fig. 9.4). A similar old tradition of living rooms heated with smoke ovens has been preserved in vernacular architecture in the Eastern Alps (e.g. Geramb 1925; 1950; Haberlandt 1937; Igl 1958). Preserved archaic block houses in Bohemia were built of thick fir logs, which were 30–40 cm thick, rested on stone foundations, and were furnished with an outer daub plaster held together by wooden pegs ensuring both heat and fire insulation. Inside the *jizba* with an area of 30–40 m², slots between individual logs were filled with moss and daub. The ceiling was also made of logs and covered with a thick layer of daub. Excavations of burnt Late Medieval rural houses revealed large assemblages of fired daub fragments with negatives of log construction, showing details of this building technique, which corresponds to standing archaic buildings where original daub plasters in many cases have not been preserved (Vařeka & Netolický 2016, 170–175). According to documentary and ethnological sources, the *jizba* was the most important part of the house, used for daily living, meal preparation, cooking, and sleeping (Macek 1991,

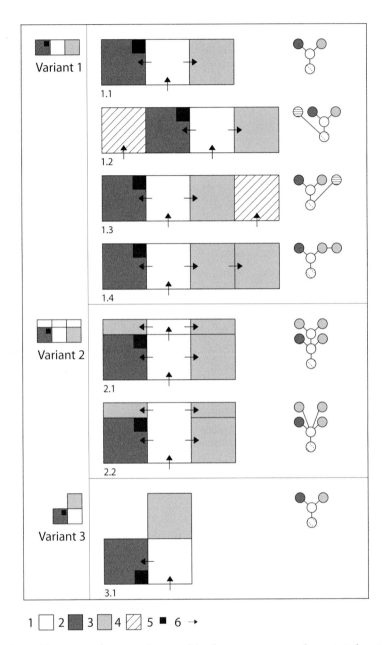

Fig. 9.3: Typology of the granary/storage sub-type of the three-compartment house in Bohemia and Moravia with access schemes. 1. entrance room 2. living room 3. granary/storage room 4. byre 5. oven 6. entrance

55–56; Petráňová & Petráň 1991, 36–37; Petráňová & Vařeka 1987, 281–282). It had no chimney, but the wooden ceiling reached a surprising height of 3.5–4.5 m, with a distinctive tarry surface. A log ceiling was supported by a transverse beam and two logs were extended over the upper part of the wall. The oven was serviced from inside

Fig. 9.4: Havlíčkův Brod. Three-compartment house of a corner timbered construction provided with a daub plaster (16th century). The jizba *(living room) with original small windows in the front, including smoke opening situated high up in the side wall. Central entrance part and storied storage part can be seen at the back (Vařeka 2004)*

the room and served for both heating and cooking or baking. The living room was furnished with small windows (50 × 50 cm) and one smaller opening situated high up, mostly in the gable wall (Škabrada 1987, 206–210; 1992, 159–161). One experiment in a reconstructed house demonstrated that smoke produced by heating was concentrated in the uppermost part of the room filling approximately 1 m below the log ceiling and left the room through a wall opening situated above a pair of windows. This allowed the room to be very amply heated with approximately 2–3 m of high smokeless space suitable for living, while only the uppermost part was filled with a constant layer of smoke (Vařeka & Netolický 2016, 175–178). Dissemination of a tile stove enabling the introduction of a *světnice* (smoke-free living room), which was operated from a corridor, the back part of which was transformed into a black kitchen, can be dated in rural milieu to the 16th century (Škabrada 2003, 27–36).

It seems that the *síň* was open to the loft and had no ceiling. These spaces were used as traffic zones but also for storage and some working activities. The ceiling height of the living room corresponds to the storey construction of the storage part of the house, often with a lower section set partly into the ground, which was used as a cellar. The 16th-century documentary and recent ethnological evidence shows that this part of the house, usually described as the *komora* (lower and upper storage room), was used for storing grain, food supplies, clothing, and tools, but was also used for sleeping. It was understood as a kind of 'safe' that had only very narrow slot windows and was always furnished with a firm lock. In some cases, the living room was the only timber part of the house and the corridor and storage area was stone-built (Petráňová & Vařeka 1987, 282–283; Škabrada 2003, 22–23).

In Upper Austria, excavations of the deserted village of Hard demonstrated that the three-compartment houses were introduced in the late 13th and 14th century. Houses with a size of 59–125 m² were very likely of a block construction and equipped with preserved stone foundations. The three-part scheme consisted of a central corridor with remains of a hearth found in numerous cases, a living room heated with an oven situated in a corner, and a storage area. Some houses had a narrow side aisle annexed into individual parts (Felgenhauer-Schmiedt 2008; Fig. 9.2: 3, 5).

In Hungary, the three-compartment houses were possibly introduced in the 14th century. According to excavations of deserted medieval villages, two areas with different constructions of the Late Medieval rural house can be defined. The traditional earth-fastened post construction was used in the eastern part of Hungary in the 14th and 15th century (Pálóczy-Horváth 2002, 309–312). Three-compartment houses consist of a *szin* (central corridor), a *szoba* (living room) furnished with a clay oven situated in a corner next door, and a *kamra* (storage room). Numerous finds of stove tiles indicate the introduction of the stove in the 15th century, which can testify for the adaption of the advanced smoke-free living room. A large clay baking oven annexed to the back wall of the corridor and remains of a hearth show that this area may have been used as a *konyha* (kitchen) (Pálóczi-Horváth 1990; 1993; Fig. 9.2: 6). A block construction resting on stone footings dominated in western Hungary. Houses with a three-compartment core were also formed by a living room with a stone oven, a central corridor, and a storage area, the lower part of which was often sunken into the ground and equipped with stone revetment and a sunken staircase. Further rooms used for storage and other purposes were linearly annexed to the house-core. Large sunken storage parts were interpreted as wine-cellars with wide entrances enabling the manipulation of barrels. Traces of open hearths on cellars floor may indicate temporary heating, ensuring the process of wine making during winter (Parádi 1979; Holl & Parádi 1982; Fig. 9.2, House 7).

Several excavations of Late Medieval villages in Slovakia have revealed evidence indicating remains of more compartment surface village houses, however the earliest direct evidence of the three-compartment house is dated to the early 16th century. The 'L'-shape building of a post-built construction is formed by a living room, a corridor, and a storage area furnished with a cellar (Hanuliak 1989; Čaplovič & Javorský 1990; Ruttkay 1999, 23–30; 2002, 269–270). There is a lack of later medieval village excavations in Poland. Recent results of non-invasive research into deserted villages in Silesia indicate that some houses may have had a three-compartment plan in the Late Medieval period (Fokt & Legut-Pintal 2016).

Formation of the three-compartment house

According to current knowledge, the three-compartment house was formed in Central Europe in the late 12th and 13th century and became the most important type of rural house in this area until the modern era. This house type seems to have appeared during a similar period, possibly with some time shifts on vast territories of diametrically different Early Medieval building traditions (Fig. 9.1). Many scholars, mostly ethnologists, archaeologists and architect-historians, have attempted to elucidate the formation of this essential type of vernacular house in eastern Central Europe. Hypotheses can be divided into two groups. The first one includes the diffusionist explanation, which claims that the three-compartment house spread to the east from other territory (southern and central Germany) or from higher social milieu (aristocratic residences and towns) as an already fully completed house (Pitterová 1965; 1976; Schier 1966). The second group espouses the autochthonous approach, which argues that this house type was formed separately in both parts of Central Europe, represented in the east by a gradual evolution from an archaic one-compartment house to a two- and later three-compartment house. The originally separate storage house (archaic Slavic *kleť*) is assumed to have been connected with the *jizba* (*izba* or dwelling house) by adding a *síň* (*sěň* or central communication area) or was simply annexed to the already existing two-compartment house, which consisted of the *jizba* and *síň* (Niederle 1913, 772–773; Moszyński 1929, 536–550; Frolec 1976; 1982; 1987). Both Late Medieval archaeological evidence and recent ethnological analogies indicate that this developmental process may have occurred in some cases. On the other hand, there is also strong evidence that some medieval rural houses were designed as three-compartment buildings, as their foundations' remains provide no proof for evolutionist building development (Smetánka 1994, 118–124).

Comparing archaeological evidence from Central Europe, it is possible to provide another explanation of the origins of the three-compartment house. Changes in rural housing appear to have been closely linked to the process of settlement transformation, villages' nucleation and stabilisation, which was connected with the adoption of a new social organization and legal and economic system that spread throughout Central Europe in the high and late Middle Ages. The dispersed and unstable Early Medieval settlement pattern was gradually superseded by a newly organized landscape with new forms of nucleated villages with regularly planned farms and surrounded with fixed laid-out field systems. Settlement pattern transformation in lowlands was accompanied by settlement expansion to hilly regions and mountain foothills (Klápště 1994, 46–50; 2004). In both western and eastern Central Europe, the first documented innovations of rural housing are of a similar character, probably with some chronological shift. Stone constructions used for house foundations made it possible to build with the perspective of a long-term continuity corresponding to both the spatial and temporal stability of transformed later medieval villages and farms. Cellars replacing the Early Medieval sunken houses and storage pits indicate changes in the means and needs for storing commodities intended for the market, and also point to a new concept of the spatial and functional organization of the farm and its built form. While the timber-framing represents innovation in building techniques in the west, corner-timbering in the east continues in the old tradition but was improved by stone foundations or combined with masonry-built parts of the house.

Many attributes of the three-compartment house type show continuity in rural house development in western Central Europe. The general concept of the house placing both dwelling and economic functions under the same roof refers to an old tradition of the long house. The size of the three-compartment house also corresponds to Early Medieval houses in southern Germany, as well as the byre part, which forms the key attribute of the byre-house. The concept of a central corridor giving access to other parts of the house might have also been derived from the longhouse tradition. However, an apparent discontinuity can be seen in the dwelling core. The older concept of living in a large hall opened to the roof space and furnished with an open hearth situated in the centre was substituted with a completely different model of living in a smaller wooden 'box' represented by a *Stube*. Archaeological evidence indicates the introduction of different heating equipment embodied by ovens in some cases which were situated in a corner or by a wall. We may suppose that an archaic form of a living 'box' provided with a *Rauchstube* (smoke oven) had been used in rural houses before the developed *Stube* with a smoke-free heating system was disseminated in the rural milieu in southern Germany. If so, we could not exclude some influences from eastern Central Europe, where this concept of a *jizba* (living room) had a long tradition.

The spatial concept of the three-compartment house, in addition to its size, represents a complete innovation in eastern Central Europe with a very different Slavic tradition of small one-compartment dwelling houses and separated storage functions and livestock-keeping in isolated buildings. The adoption of this house type changed the perception of a strict spatial separation of a single purpose dwelling house and other farm buildings with economic functions. Yet, the three-compartment core of the granary/storage-house did not include a byre, which persistently represented a separate area annexed to the house without any direct access or formed a separate wing of the farm. This strong tradition of accommodating people and livestock separately, deriving from the Early Medieval farm concept, was strictly followed until the 20th century. Interesting evidence of this perception was documented in border regions of former Czechoslovakia that were settled by new communities of mostly Czechs and Slovaks after 1945 when the original German population was deported. New settlers moving into old byre-type houses in the Sudetenland countryside immediately blocked the door connecting the corridor to the byre in order to keep livestock separately (the byre could then be accessed only from the yard; Heroldová & Matějová 1990, 267). Thus, these buildings lost one of the main attributes of the byre-house and became two-compartment houses in terms of access and communication.

On the other hand, there is a continuity in the concept of the living room represented by a small, well-insulated wooden 'box' with an effective oven heater, which is adapted to the Central and eastern European climate. It seems that the archaic Slavic one-compartment dwelling *izba* was incorporated into the three-compartment house as its living part without much alteration in eastern Central Europe, keeping its name and formal attributes such as size, the internal arrangement with a large oven situated in a corner next to the door, and its block construction.

Conclusion

Instead of diffusion or autochthonous hypothesis, it is possible to introduce a new explanation regarding the three-compartment house formation. Comparing the Early Medieval building tradition and a new built form, we find identical and different attributes in both parts of Central Europe. The concept of housing both the dwelling and economic zones under the same roof represents a continuity in western Central Europe but a radical discontinuity in eastern Central Europe and vice versa; the model of a living room as a comparatively small, well-heated and insulated wooden 'box' is a continuity in building culture in the east but a sharp discontinuity in the west. Separation or contact between people and livestock in the house expressed by two sub-types of the three-compartment house, the byre-house and the granary/storage-house, can be understood as a continuation of the two different archaic perceptions of dwelling within a new built form. Medieval Central Europe, with a long tradition of close contacts between the Germanic and Slavic world, might be seen as an area of mutual cultural influence. The formation of the three-compartment house may have represented one of the results of this cultural exchange and reciprocal borrowings. It may be interpreted as a synthesis of different traditions that took shape in the transformation of the built environment.

Bibliography

Atzbach, R. (2014) The 'stube' and its heating. Archaeological evidence for a smoke-free living room between Alps and North Sea. In M. S. Kristiansen & K. Giles (eds.) *Dwellings, Identities and Homes. European Housing Culture from the Viking Age to the Renaissance*, 195–209. Aarhus, Aarhus University Press.

Bedal, K. (1993) *Historische Hausforschung. Eine Einführung in Arbeitsweise, Begriffe und Literatur*. Bad Windsheim, Fränkische Freilandmuseum Bad Windsheim.

Bedal, K. (1998) Vielfältig und Vielräumig. Bemerkungen zum spätmittelalterlichen bäuerlichen Hausbau in Nordbayern – Bestand, Formen und Befunde. In K. Bedal, S. Fechter, & H. Heidrich (eds.) *Haus und Kultur im Spätmittelalter, Quellen und Materialien zur Hausforschung in Bayern 10*, 75–127. Bad Windsheim, Fränkische Freilandmuseum Bad Windsheim.

Bedal, K. (2002) Spätmittelalterlicher bäuerlicher Hausbau in Süddeutschland. Versuch eines Überblicks – Bestand, Formen und Befunde. In J. Klápště (ed.) *Ruralia 4, Památky archeologické - Supplementum 15*, 240–256. Prague, Institute of Archaeology, Academy of Sciences of the Czech Republic.

Belcredi, L. (2006) *Bystřec. O založení, životě a zániku středověké vsi*. Brno, Muzejní a vlastivědná společnost v Brně and Moravské zemské muzeum.

Buko, A. (2006) *Archeologia Polski wczesnośredniowiecznej*. Warszawa, Wydawnictwo Trio.

Čaplovič, D. &Javorský, F. (1990) Najnovšie poznatky o vývoji stredovekého dedinského domu na Spiši. *Nové obzory* 31, 63–120.

Chudziak, W. (1987) Z badań nad budownictwem drewnianym Wielkopolski w okresie wczesnego średniowiecza. *Sprawozdania Archeologiczne* 39, 343–346.

Donat, P. (1980) *Haus, Hof und Dorf in Mitteleuropa vom 7. bis 12. Jahrhundert. Archäologische Beiträge zur Entwicklung und Struktur der bäuerlichen Siedlung*. Berlin, Akademie-Verlag (Schriften zur Ur- und Frühgeschichte 33).

Donat, P. (1993) Zehn Keller von Gebesee, Kr. Erfurt. Studien zu hochmittelalterlichen Kelleranlagen. *Alt - Thüringen* 27, 207–264.

Donat, P. (1995) Neuere archäologische und bauhistorische Forschungsergebnisse zum ländlichen Hausbau des 11. – 13. Jahrhunderts in Mittel- und Süddeutschland. *Germania* 73, 421–439.

Dušek, S. (1983) *Geschichte und Kultur der Slawen in Thüringen.* Weimar, Museum für Ur- und Frühgeschichte Thüringens.

Ernst, E. & Klápště, J. (1993) Stahlnhain – eine untergegangene Waldschmiedesiedlung, *Hessische Heimat* 43, 43–50.

Fehring, G. P. (1973) Zur archäologischen Erforschung mittelalterlicher Dorfsiedlungen in Südwestdeutschland. *Zeitschrift für Agrargeschichte und Agrarsoziologie* 21, 1–35.

Felgenhauer-Schmiedt, S. (2008) *Hard. Ein Wüstungskomplex bei Thaya im niederösterreichschen Waldviertel.* Archäologische Forschungen in Niederösterreich 6. St. Pölten, NÖ Instituts für Landeskunde.

Fokt, K. & Legut-Pintal, M. (2016) Zanikłe wsie Wzgórz Strzelińskich: stan in perspektywy badań. In P. Nocuń, A. Przybyła-Dumin & K. Fokt (eds.) *Wieś zaginiona. Stan i perspektywy badań*, 113–146. Chorzów, Muzeum „Górnośląski Park Etnograficzny w Chorzowie".

Frolec, V. (1976) Pokus o etnografickou interpretaci archeologických výzkumů středověké zemědělské usedlosti. *Archaeologia historica* 1, 49–52.

Frolec, V. (1982) K interpretaci geneze trojdílného komorového domu (Ve světle archeologických výzkumů na jihozápadní Moravě). *Archaeologia historica* 7, 67–77.

Frolec, V. (1987) Vesnická stavební kultura mezi středověkem a novověkem. *Archaeologia historica* 12, 47–83.

Geramb, V. (1925) Die geographische Verbreitung und Dichte der ostalpinen Rauchstuben. *Wiener Zeitschrift für Volkskunde* 30, 70–123.

Geramb, V. (1950) *Die Rauchstuben im Lande Salzburg.Beitrag zur Hausforschung der Ostalpenländer.* Salzburg, Institut für Volkskunde Salzburg.

Gringmuth-Dallmer, E. (1999) Altlandschaft und Altsiedlung zwischen Elbe/Saale und Oder/Neiße. In K. Fehn, H. Bender, K. Brandt, D. Denecke, H-R. Egli, E. Gringmuth-Dallmer, F. Irsigler, M. Müller-Wille, H-J. Nitz, G. Oberbeck & W. Schich (eds.) *Siedlungsforschung. Archäologie - Geschichte - Geographie* 17, 255–268. Bonn, Verlag Siedlungsforschung Bonn.

Haberlandt, A. (1937) Die Rauchstube eines alten Einheitshauses im Kitzbühler Lande. *Wiener Zeitschrift für Volkskunde* 42, 89–95.

Hanuliak, M. (1989) Praveké, včasnodejinné a stredoveké osídlenie v Chľabe. *Slovenská archeológia* 37, 151–212.

Heroldová, I. & Matějová, V. (1990) Novoosídlenecké pohraničí. *Západočeská vlastivěda. Národopis*, 263–290. Plzeň, Západočeské nakladatelství.

Herrmann, J. (1981) *Zwischen Hradschin und Vineta. Frühe Kulturen der Westslawen.* Leipzig, Urania Verlag.

Holl, I. & Parádi, N. (1982) *Das mittelalterliche Dorf Sarvaly.* Budapest, Akadémiai Kiadó.

Igl, K. (1958) Zur Verbreitung der Rauchstube in Nordtirol. *Österreichische Zeitschrift für Volkskunde* 61, 141–145.

Kenzler, H. (2002) Hausbau in Breunsdorf bei Leipzig. Von der „Kolonization" bis in die frühe Neuzeit. In J. Klápště (ed.) *Ruralia 4, Památky archeologické - Supplementum 15*, 101–110. Prague, Institute of Archaeology, Academy of Sciences of the Czech Republic.

Klápště, J. (1994) Změna - středověká transformace a její předpoklady. In J. Klápště & P. Vařeka (eds.) *Mediaevalia Archaeologica Bohemica 1993, Památky archeologické - Supplementum 2*, 9–59. Prague, Institute of Archaeology, Academy of Sciences of the Czech Republic.

Klápště, J. (2004) *Proměny českých zemí ve středověku.* Praha, Nakladatelství Lidové noviny.

Klír, T. (2016) Zaniklé středověké vsi ve výzkumném záměru Ústavu pro archeologii Univerzity Karlovy v Praze. Zaniklý Spindelbach (Krušné Hory), Kří a Hol (střední Čechy). In P. Nocuń, A.

Przybyła-Dumin & K. Fokt (eds.) *Wieś zaginiona. Stan i perspektywy badań*, 17–58. Chorzów, Muzeum „Górnośląski Park Etnograficzny w Chorzowie".

Losert, H. (2012) Die Slawen in Nordostbayern. In M. Chytráček, H. Gruber, J. Michálek, R. Sandner & K. Schmotz (eds.) *Fines Transire 21. Archäologische Arbeitsgemeinschaft Ostbayern/West- und Südböhmen/Oberösterreich*, 139–168. Rahden, Verlag Marie Leidorf.

Macek, J (1991) K sémantice středověkého domu a jeho vnitřního členění. In *Husitský Tábor 10*, 47–66. Tábor, Muzeum husitského revolučního hnutí v Táboře.

Měchurová, Z. (1997) *Konůvky - zaniklá středověká ves ve Ždánickém lese. Srovnávací analýza nálezového fondu ze zaniklé středověké vsi Konůvky, kat. Heršpice, okr. Vyškov. Studie Archeologického ústavu AVČR v Brně 17/1*. Brno, Archeologický ústav AVČR v Brně.

Meduna, P. (1992) K vnitřní struktuře raně středověkých sídlišť. *Archaeologia historica 17*, 281–290.

Molnár, E. (2011) Régészeti és geofyzikai kutatások eredményei Esztergom-Szidódon. In B. Koloszi & K. Szilágy (eds.) *Sötét idők falvai. 2006-ban Debrecen megrendezett konferencia 2 kötete*, 671–685. Debrecen, Tegeszeti tár Hajdú-Bihar megyei múzeumok igazgatósága.

Moszyński, K. (1929) *Kultura ludowa Słowian I. Kultura materjalna*. Kraków, Polska Akademia umjętności.

Moździoch, S. (1996) Das mittelalterliche Dorf in Polen im Lichte der archäologischen Forschung. In J. Fridrich, J. Klápště, Z. Smetánka & P. Sommer (eds.) *Ruralia 1, Památky archeologické - Supplementum 5*, 282–295. Prague, Institute of Archaeology, Academy of Sciences of the Czech Republic.

Nekuda, R. & Nekuda, V. (1997) *Mstěnice 2. Zaniklá středověká ves. Dům a dvůr ve středověké vesnici.* Brno, Muzejní a vlastivědná společnost v Brně.

Nekuda, V. (1975) *Pfaffenschlag. Zaniklá středověká ves u Slavonic.* Brno, Muzejní a vlastivědná společnost v Brně.

Nováček, K. & Vařeka, P. (1996) Archaeological research of present – day villages of a medieval origin in Bohemia. In J. Fridrich, J. Klápště, Z. Smetánka & P. Sommer (eds.) *Ruralia 1, Památky archeologické - Supplementum 5*, 314–325. Prague, Institute of Archaeology Academy of Sciences of the Czech Republic.

Pálóczi-Horváth, A. (1990) Agrártörteneti emlékek a középkori Szentkirály faluban. *A Magyar mezögazdaság múzeum közleményei 1988-1989*, 69–94.

Pálóczi-Horváth, A. (1993) Structures du village medieval de Szentkirály de 15e – 16e siècles. In J. Pavúk (ed.) *Actes du XIIe Congrès International des Sciences Préhistoriques et Protohistoriques 4*, 113–118. Bratislava, Institut archeologique de l'Academie Slovaque des Sciences a Nitra.

Pálóczi-Horváth, A. (2002) Development of the Late – Medieval house in Hungary. In J. Klápště (ed.) *Ruralia 4, Památky archeologické - Supplementum 15*, 308–319. Prague, Institute of Archaeology, Academy of Sciences of the Czech Republic.

Parádi, N. (1979) Die Keller und Öffen der mittelalterlichen Orschaft Sarvaly. *Archaeologiai Értesítő 106*, 65–76.

Petráňová, L. & Petráň, J. (1991) Středověké lexikografie k názvosloví domu a jeho příslušenství. In *Husitský Tábor 10*, 17–46. Tábor, Muzeum husitského revolučního hnutí v Táboře.

Petráňová, L. & Vařeka, J. (1987) Vybavení venkovské zemědělské usedlosti v době předbělohorské (na pozadí poddanských inventářů). *Archaeologia historica 12*, 277–286.

Pitterová, A. (1965) Vývoj základních půdorysných typů tradičního domu na území ČSSR ve světle archeologických pramenů. *Český lid 52*, 275–295.

Pitterová, A. (1976) Vztah vesnického a městského domu. *Český lid 63*, 204–217.

Pražák, V. (1958) K problematice základních půdorysných typů lidových staveb v Československu. *Československá etnografie 6*, 275–295.

Rückert, P. (1988) Archäologisch – historische Forschungen in einer Mittelalterlichen Wüstung bei Eichenfürst. *Das archäologische Jahr in Bayern 1987*, 179–181.

Ruttkay, M. (1998) Dedina a dom vo vrcholnom a neskorom stredoveku. In J. Botík (ed.) *Ľudová architektúra a urbanizmus vidieckych sídiel na Slovensku z pohľadu najnovších poznatkov archeológie a etnografie*, 37–66. Bratislava, Academic Electronic Press.

Ruttkay, M. (1999) Výskum stredovekých dedinských sídlisk na Slovensku (stav a perspektivy). *Archaeologia historica* 14, 7–40.

Ruttkay, M. (2002) Der ländliche Hausbau des 5. bis 15. Jh. im nördlichen Karpatenbecken (Slowakei). In J. Klápště (ed.) *Ruralia 4, Památky archeologické - Supplementum 15*, 264–271. Prague, Institute of Archaeology, Academy of Sciences of the Czech Republic.

Šaurová, D. (1977) Vilémov - zaniklá středověká vesnice na úpatí Drahanské vrchoviny. In M. Richter (ed.) *Středověká archeologie a studium počátků měst*, 264–271. Praha, Archeologický ústav ČSAV.

Schier, B. (1966) *Hauslandschaften und Kulturbewegungen im östlichen Mitteleuropa*. Göttingen, Verlag Otto Schwarz & Co.

Schmidt, E. (1986) Die bauliche Entwicklung vom Grubenhaus zum unterkellerten Wohngebäude in der Wüstung Sülchen auf der Gemarkung Rottenburg, Kreis Tübingen. *Archäologische Ausgrabungen in Baden Württemberg* 1985, 201–203.

Schreg, R. (2002) Haus und Hof im Rahmen der Dorfgenese. Zum Wandel der Bauform in Süddeutschland. In J. Klápště (ed.) *Ruralia 4, Památky archeologické - Supplementum 15*, 111–122. Prague, Institute of Archaeology Academy of Sciences of the Czech Republic.

Schreg, R. (2012) Farmsteads in early medieval Germany – architecture and organisation. In J. A. Q. Castillo (ed.) *Arquelogía de la arquitectura y arquitectura del espacio doméstico en la alta Edad Mediea Europea*, 247–265. Madrid, Ehupress (Arquelogía de la arquitectura 9).

Škabrada, J. (1987) Poznámky k pokračujícímu průzkumu domu čp. 2 v Lučici (Ke vzniku středověkého domu s trojdílným půdorysem). *Archaeologia historica* 12, 203–213.

Škabrada, J. (1992) K charakteru výstavby vesnického domu 16. a 17. století v Čechách. In J. Škabrada (ed.) *Vesnický dům v 16. a 17. století*, 138–167. Praha, České vysoké učení technické.

Škabrada, J. (2003) *Lidové stavby. Architektura českého venkova*. Praha, Argo.

Smetánka, Z. (1988) *Život středověké vesnice. Zaniklá Svídna*. Praha, Academia.

Smetánka, Z. (1994) K problematice trojdílného domu v Čechách a na Moravě v období vrcholného a pozdního středověku, In J. Klápště & P. Vařeka (eds.), *Mediaevalia Archaeologica Bohemica 1993, Památky archeologické - Supplementum 2*, 117–138. Praha, Archeologický ústav Akademie věd České republiky.

Takács, M. (1998) Dörfliche Siedlungen der Árpádenzeit (10.–13. Jh.) in Westungarn. In J. Fridrich, J. Klápště, Z. Smetánka & P. Sommer (eds.) *Ruralia 2, Památky archeologické - Supplementum 11*, 181–191. Prague, Institute of Archaeology Academy of Sciences of the Czech Republic.

Takács, M. (2002) Der Hausbau in Ungarn vom 2. bis zum 13. Jahrhundert n. Chr. – ein Zeitalter einheitlicher Grubenhäuser ?. In J. Klápště (ed.) *Ruralia 4, Památky archeologické - Supplementum 15*, 272–290. Prague, Institute of Archaeology Academy of Sciences of the Czech Republic.

Timpel, W. (1982) *Gommerstedt. Eine hochmittelalterliche Herrensitz in Thüringen*. Weimar, Museum für Ur- und Frühgeschichte Thüringens.

Vařeka, P. (1991) Příspěvek k problematice vypovídacích možností konstrukčních reliktů středověkého vesnického domu. *Archeologické rozhledy* 43, 585–592.

Vařeka, P. (2004) *Archeologie středověkého domu I: Proměny vesnického obydlí v Evropě v průběhu staletí (6.–15. století)*. Plzeň, Archaeologica.

Vařeka, P. (2013) Příspěvek k podobě vesnického domu ze sklonku středověku na Českobudějovicku. Soubor mazanic s otisky konstrukcí z Češnovic. *Archeologické výzkumy v jižních Čechách* 26, 207–236.

Vařeka, P., Holata, L., Rožmberský, P. & Schejbalová, Z. (2011) Středověké osídlení Rokycanska a problematika zaniklých vsí. *Archaeologia historica* 36, 319–342.

Vařeka, P., Kostrouch, F., Kočár, P. & Sůvová, Z. (2010) Příspěvek ke studiu žijících vsí středověkého původu. Pozůstatky zástavby z pozdního středověku na parcele č.p. 121 v Mikulčicích. *Přehled výzkumů* 51, 249–265.

Vařeka, P. & Netolický, P. (2016) Die Rekonstruktion eines spätmittelalterlichen Dorfhauses im archäologischen Park Prag-Liboc. In O. Chvojka, M. Chytráček, H. Gruber, L. Husty, J. Michálek, R. Sandner, K. Schmotz and S. Traxler (eds.) *Fines Transire 25. Archäologische Arbeitsgemeinschaft Ostbayern/West- und Südböhmen/Oberösterreich*, 167–180. Rahden, Verlag Marie Leidorf.

Zimmermann, W. H. (1998) Pfosten, Ständer und Schwelle und der Übergang vom Pfosten- zum Ständerbau. Eine Studie zu Innovation und Beharrung im Hausbau. Zu Konstruktion und Haltbarkeit prähistorischer bis neuzeitlicher Holzbauten von den Nord- und Ostseeländern bis zu den Alpen. *Probleme der Küstenforschung* 25, 9–241.